ORCA
WILD

BEAVERS

RADICAL RODENTS AND ECOSYSTEM ENGINEERS

FRANCES BACKHOUSE

ORCA BOOK PUBLISHERS

Library and Archives Canada Cataloguing in Publication
Title: Beavers : radical rodents and ecosystem
engineers / Frances Backhouse.
Names: Backhouse, Frances, author.
Series: Orca wild.
Description: Series statement: Orca wild |
Includes bibliographical references and index.
Identifiers: Canadiana (print) 20200336819 |
Canadiana (ebook) 20200336932 |
ISBN 9781459824690 (hardcover) |
ISBN 9781459824706 (PDF) | ISBN 9781459824713 (EPUB)
Subjects: LCSH: Beavers—Juvenile literature. |
LCSH: Beavers—Ecology—Juvenile literature.
Classification: LCC QL737.R632 B32 2021 | DDC j599.37—dc23

Library of Congress Control Number: 2020944963

Summary: Part of the Orca Wild series, this nonfiction
book for middle-grade readers explores the important role
beavers play as a keystone species. They were nearly driven
to extinction for their furs, but today beavers are valued
for their role as habitat creators and water stewards.

Orca Book Publishers is committed to reducing
the consumption of nonrenewable resources in the
making of our books. We make every effort to use
materials that support a sustainable future.

Orca Book Publishers gratefully acknowledges the support
for its publishing programs provided by the following
agencies: the Government of Canada, the Canada Council
for the Arts and the Province of British Columbia through
the BC Arts Council and the Book Publishing Tax Credit.

For a complete list of references, visit the
page for this book at orcabook.com.

Front cover photos by George Lepp/Getty Images
Back cover photo by Moment of Perception
Photography/Getty Images
Edited by Kirstie Hudson
Design by Dahlia Yuen

Printed and bound in China.

24 23 22 21 • 1 2 3 4

A peaceful beaver pond is a great place to pause and enjoy nature. BRUCE CAMPOS/GETTY IMAGES

For all the special kits in my widespread colony:
Jake, Claire, Amelia, Max and Wren.

CONTENTS

Introduction   1

1.
THE MIGHTY BEAVER

Meet the Mighty Beaver   5
Beaver Geography   6
Four-Legged Lumberjacks   7
Dam Good Engineers   10
Home Sweet Home   13
A Well-Designed Rodent   14
Teeth and Tails   18
Castorid Communications   19
Territorial Marking and a Cure for Headaches   21
Kits Have It Easy   22
Growing Up and Moving On   23
Tree Bark, Poop and Other Tasty Snacks   27
Winter Dining   30

2.
HABITAT MAKERS AND COMMUNITY CREATORS

Tiiim-ber!!   35
Master Builders at Work   39
No Leaks Allowed   44
Lodge Logistics   45
Dig This   50
Beavers on Bulldozers   51
Keystone Connections   52

3.
FROM SLAUGHTER TO SALVATION

Beaverland   59

Brown Gold   61

Fur-Trade Wipeout   62

Disrupted Traditions   64

Bouncing Back   66

A Change of Heart   68

Happy Landings   74

From Rare to Raring to Go   77

Justin Beaver Moves to the City   78

4.
LIVING WITH BEAVERS

The Trouble with Beavers   83

Too Close for Comfort   84

Reservoirs, Speed Bumps and Water Filters   86

Coexistence Means Everyone Wins   88

Trick or Treat   92

Tree-Sharing Tactics   99

Kick-Starter Dams   101

Watching Beavers in the Wild   105

Signs and Tracks   106

A Day to Celebrate Beavers   107

How Can You Give Beavers a Boost?   111

Glossary   114

Resources   116

Acknowledgments   118

Index   120

While making a radio documentary about beavers, I recorded audio at this beaver pond in Alberta. The sounds included birds singing, frogs calling, insects buzzing and beavers slapping their tails.
PIERRE BOLDUC

INTRODUCTION

Beavers are kind of goofy-looking. They have big orange buckteeth, front feet that don't match their back ones and a tail that looks like it was run over by a tractor. Yet those odd features are all part of what makes this animal so remarkable. The beaver is North America's number one *ecosystem engineer* and an essential *keystone species*. I'm always excited when I get to see beavers in action.

One of my most memorable beaver-watching experiences took place in Algonquin Provincial Park in Ontario. Evening is a good time to spot beavers, so I set off along the Beaver Pond Trail just before sunset. My destination was a massive dam that curved across one end of Amikeus Lake, halfway around the trail loop. Earlier that day I had hiked past the dam and seen a trickle of water flowing over it. No beavers were around then, but I thought they might come to deal with that trickle in the evening. When I reached the dam, I found a comfortable seat on a log. I knew I might be waiting for a while.

Five minutes passed. And then five more minutes. Suddenly I noticed the V-shaped wake of a small dark object moving across the lake. As it got closer, I started to make out its features. First the knobby ears. Then the

A swimming beaver is like an iceberg—most of its mass is hidden underwater.
GARYSFRP/GETTY IMAGES

small black eyes. And finally the flaring nostrils. When the beaver had paddled almost to the shore, it started cruising back and forth in front of me. Peering down into the water, I saw how it steered with its tail and propelled itself with slow kicks of its big webbed hind feet, first one foot and then the other.

The beaver was also observing me, and maybe it was talking to me. Several times it emitted a low, rumbling sound, like a cross between a growl and a purr. It was too bad I didn't speak its language.

My new acquaintance then swam over to the dam and clambered onto it. It waddled along the top of the dam, seemingly unconcerned by the trickling water. After pausing for a moment to munch on a bush, it belly flopped back into the lake and paddled away.

When the beaver reached the shore opposite me, it emerged again. It sat upright on the bank with its tail folded underneath its rotund body and began to groom itself. I watched through my binoculars as the beaver ran its front paws down its chest, belly and sides, pressing water out of its thick coat. Once it had dried off, it spent several minutes rubbing waterproofing oil from its oil glands into its coat. Now and then it paused for some vigorous scratching.

This was the first time I had ever watched a beaver groom itself, so I was excited. It felt like sneaking into my favorite singer's dressing room and watching her do her hair and makeup before a big show. Eventually the beaver slipped back into the pond and glided away. By then it was almost dark. I put on my headlamp and made my way back along the forested path to the parking lot.

Over the years I've heard a lot of beaver stories. Stories about encounters with beavers. Stories Indigenous Peoples have handed down from generation to generation. Stories told by scientists who study these animals. Stories about how the fur trade almost drove beavers to extinction and how they were saved. And stories from people who are working to figure out how we humans can get along better with beavers in the modern world.

Maybe you have a beaver story too. Or maybe yours is still out there, waiting for you to find it.

Beavers often dive immediately after slapping their tails. Water fountains up as the beaver kicks its hind feet in the air and plunges below the surface.
CHUCK GARRETT

1
THE MIGHTY BEAVER

MEET THE MIGHTY BEAVER

Beavers are amazing. They can build structures that are visible from outer space. They can turn streams into lakes and change the shape of valleys. They can gnaw right through the trunks of trees that are as tall as flagpoles. And they do all of this with nothing more than their sharp front teeth, nimble paws and powerful muscles.

There are only two kinds of beavers in the world today, the North American and the Eurasian. Scientists also have fancier names for them. They call the North American beaver *Castor canadensis* and the Eurasian beaver *Castor fiber*. You probably noticed that both names start with the word *Castor*. That tells us that these two *species* are closely related—kind of like cousins.

Unlike most human cousins, *Castor canadensis* and *Castor fiber* look nearly identical. The only sure way to tell them apart is to examine their *DNA*—the coding instructions for life that every animal and plant carries in its cells. DNA analysis shows that the two species of beaver have slightly

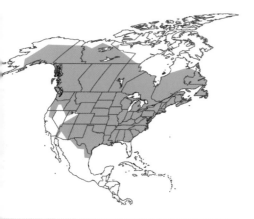

The North American beaver's historical range. Before 1500, *Castor canadensis* inhabited almost every part of the continent where there was wood and water.
THE BEAVER DISTRIBUTION MAP, HINTERLAND WHO'S WHO, CANADIAN WILDLIFE SERVICE, ENVIRONMENT CANADA. REPRODUCED WITH PERMISSION OF THE MINISTER OF PUBLIC WORKS AND GOVERNMENT SERVICES, 2005.

Humans have significantly changed the beaver's world over the past 500 years.
PHILIPPE HENRY / DESIGN PICS/GETTY IMAGES

different genetic blueprints. Nevertheless, they do all the same beaverish things, like felling trees and building dams. This book is mostly about *Castor canadensis*, but a mighty beaver is a mighty beaver no matter where it lives.

BEAVER GEOGRAPHY

In ancient times Eurasian beavers were common throughout Europe, northern Asia and Great Britain. Unfortunately, humans nearly drove them to extinction. By the 1600s there were no more beavers in Britain. In Europe and Asia their numbers hit bottom around 1900. At that point, only about 1,200 Eurasian beavers remained, mostly living in remote parts of Scandinavia, Russia and Mongolia. Today the Eurasian beaver is making a comeback across much of its range.

The North American beaver's homeland is—you guessed it—North America. Long ago beavers populated almost every corner of what we now call Canada and the United States, plus a sliver of northern Mexico. Their domain stretched from the Atlantic coast to the Pacific coast and from just south of the Rio Grande all the way to the northern tree line. In a few places it even reached the Arctic Ocean. Pretty much the only parts of North America without beavers were those with no trees

or shrubs—hot, dry deserts, alpine areas high in the mountains, and the *Arctic tundra*. Most of the Florida peninsula was also off-limits. Too many hungry alligators lurk in the swamps there.

Back then this continent was home to tens of millions of beavers. Or maybe hundreds of millions—no one knows for sure. We do know that Indigenous Peoples had been sharing this continent with beavers for a very long time before Europeans showed up in the late 1400s and that the newcomers rapidly reduced the number of beavers.

FOUR-LEGGED LUMBERJACKS

Beavers are famous for doing two things that no other animals (except humans) ever do. They cut down trees, and they build dams. These two activities are closely connected, because before beavers can start building a dam, they have to gather their construction materials.

Although beavers are sometimes active during the day, they usually work the night shift, starting near dusk and quitting as the sun rises. Their *nocturnal* habits make it hard to see them in action. But if you go for a walk in any beaver neighborhood, you'll find signs of their work. Felled trees are hard to miss, and their stumps have an unmistakable shape—they look like the pointy end of a pencil.

Building isn't the only thing beavers have in mind when they cut down trees. Their first priority is dinner (or lunch or breakfast). Beavers eat many things, but their most important food is *cambium*—the soft, nutritious layer of bark that lies between the hard inner wood and the tough outer bark. After they've eaten the edible parts of a tree, including the twigs and leaves, they use the trunk and branches to build their dams and *lodges*.

Parallel, tooth-sized grooves in the wood of these aspen stumps are a sure sign that a beaver cut them down.
FRANCES BACKHOUSE

For beavers, the inner bark of a freshly cut tree is delicious and nutritious food.
FRANCES BACKHOUSE

BEAVER TALES
ANCIENT ANCESTORS

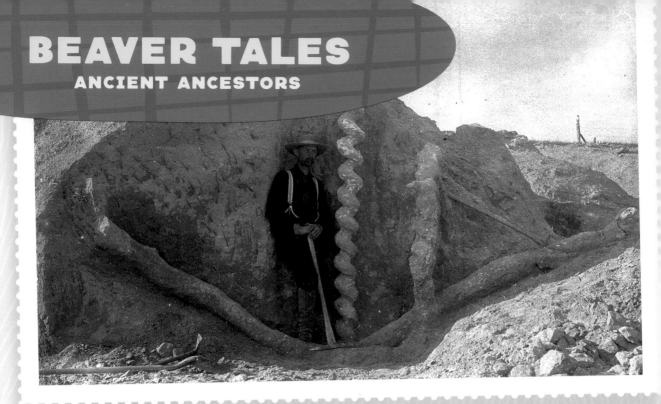

Paleontologist Frederick C. Kenyon stands beside the fossilized spiral-shaped burrow of an extinct beaver called *Paleocastor* in 1892. The site of this excavation is now part of Agate Fossil Beds National Monument in Nebraska.
ERWIN H. BARBOUR, MUSEUM DIRECTOR PAPERS, ARCHIVES & SPECIAL COLLECTIONS, UNIVERSITY OF NEBRASKA-LINCOLN LIBRARIES

THE BEAVER FAMILY got its start in North America about 37 million years ago. Although there are only two beaver species alive today, dozens of others have come and gone. Some of these now-extinct beavers inhabited dry, treeless grasslands. Others were **semi-aquatic**, like modern beavers. Very few of them cut wood with their teeth or built dams.

Several years ago I visited the Canadian Museum of Nature to learn more about ancient beavers from Natalia Rybczynski. She's a paleobiologist—a scientist who studies fossil plants and animals. Natalia got her start in paleobiology when she was 16, in this same museum, as part of a high school mentorship program.

One of the beavers Natalia studies is called *Dipoides*. It lived in the Arctic millions of years ago, when the climate was warmer and forests grew in the Far North. Down in the museum's storage rooms, Natalia opened a cabinet and pulled out a drawer filled with fossilized *Dipoides* bones and teeth. She and other researchers dug them up on Ellesmere Island, which is only about 500 miles (804 kilometers) from

the North Pole. They've also unearthed lots of sticks with *Dipoides* tooth marks on them. During my visit she showed me some four-million-year-old sticks with gnawed ends— the oldest beaver-cut wood ever found.

The largest beaver that roamed the earth was at least as big as a Saint Bernard dog. Its scientific name is *Castoroides*, but most people call it the giant beaver. When Natalia handed me one of this beaver's incisors, I was surprised by its size and weight. It was nearly 6 inches (15 centimeters) long and as heavy as a brick. That's partly because tooth enamel is the hardest material in the body, Natalia explained.

My favorite extinct castorid is *Paleocastor*. These prairie-dog-sized beavers used their teeth and long claws to dig vertical shafts that spiraled 6 to 10 feet (2 to 3 meters) down to their underground burrows. Some of the diggings eventually filled with sand and solidified into **trace fossils**. It's hard to believe these rock-hard corkscrews were made by relatives of modern beavers, but fossilized *Paleocastor* bones found inside them confirm their origins.

Summer on Ellesmere Island in Nunavut can be cold and wet. That didn't keep Natalia Rybczynski (on the left) and her research assistant from their work at this prehistoric beaver pond.
MARTIN LIPMAN

The giant beaver's big, blunt teeth were no good for cutting down trees or gnawing bark. This ancient animal mostly ate soft, succulent pond weeds.
FRANCES BACKHOUSE

DAM GOOD ENGINEERS

They don't wear hard hats or carry calculators, but beavers are among the animal world's most talented ecosystem engineers. Their most impressive engineering skill is building dams. Just like the dams humans build, beaver dams are designed to hold back flowing water. Depending on where it's located, a beaver dam can widen a stream channel and create a new pond or make an existing pond bigger. Dam building is hard work, but it's worth the effort for beavers, because water is their safe place.

The beaver's most feared enemies are land animals, including wolves, coyotes, cougars and bears. If they meet one of these predators onshore, their chances of escaping on foot are slim. Beavers can gallop for a short distance if necessary, but their normal gait is a slow waddle. A cornered beaver is also unlikely to win a fight, even though

Wolves are one of the beaver's main predators. ADAM JONES/GETTY IMAGES

The water on the upstream side of a beaver dam is usually noticeably higher than on the downstream side. FRANCES BACKHOUSE

its tree-cutting *incisors* can slash like a knife. Despite the risk of getting eaten, beavers have to venture onto land sometimes to gather food and building materials. When they do, they always try to stay close to water so they have an escape route.

If beavers cut down all the trees and shrubs near the water's edge faster than they can grow back, their overland journeys become longer and riskier. When that happens, they use their engineering skills to reduce their commuting distance and the risk of running into predators along the way. By raising the height of existing dams or building new ones, beavers can flood more land and create safe access to new logging zones.

All beavers know how to construct these incredible feats of engineering, but some beaver neighborhoods don't have dams. They're unnecessary in large lakes and impossible to build across very wide rivers.

11

After eating the bark, beavers use peeled sticks for building. Bright white sticks are a sign of recent activity. Over time they will fade to gray.
FRANCES BACKHOUSE

HOME SWEET HOME

Beavers also use their engineering expertise to construct lodges—dome-shaped dwellings that shelter them from harsh weather and protect them from predators. Lodges are family homes where beaver kits are born and raised and beavers of all ages rest, sleep and sometimes eat.

When people talk about beaver lodges, they're usually referring to the kind that is completely surrounded by water. Like a castle encircled by a moat, a freestanding lodge provides high-security housing for beavers. But some locations aren't suitable for this kind of construction. Beavers that live in wide, fast-flowing rivers or deep lakes have to settle for a home that is anchored to land on one side—either a *bank den* or bank lodge.

A bank den is a simple burrow dug into the bank of a river or lake, often underneath tree roots to make it harder for predators to bust through the roof. Bank dens are usually temporary homes. For more permanent and secure accommodation, beavers can convert a bank den into a bank lodge by piling sticks on top and plastering the exterior with mud.

This large bank lodge on the edge of the Yukon River provides warm, safe, year-round accommodation for its inhabitants. FRANCES BACKHOUSE

DAM

ICE

FOOD CACHE

VENTILATION HOLE

LODGE

LIVING QUARTERS

FEEDING PLATFORM

Whether a lodge is surrounded by water or built on a bank, its doorways will be hidden below the surface. Most lodges have at least two underwater entrances. From each entrance a short tunnel rises to a feeding platform that sits just above the waterline. A more spacious opening sits above the feeding platform and functions as the family's shared living room and bedroom. Wood chips and shredded vegetation carpet the floor of this higher and drier chamber.

A WELL-DESIGNED RODENT

Beavers are rodents, just like mice, rats, squirrels and hamsters, but they're much bigger than most of their relatives. A typical adult beaver measures about 3 feet (1 meter) from nose to tail tip and weighs 35 to 70 pounds (16 to 32 kilograms). Beavers never stop growing, so the older the individual, the bigger it will be. The heftiest tip the scales at around 100 pounds (45 kilograms). Those burly beavers might even outweigh you or some of your friends.

A beaver's eyes, ears and nose are all positioned near the top of its head so it can see, hear and smell when swimming. JENNIFER VANDERHOOF

Beavers come in many shades of brown, from almost black to pale cream. Medium brown is the most common fur color.
SYLVIE BOUCHARD/GETTY IMAGES

From head to toes to tail, beavers are magnificently adapted for their semi-aquatic lifestyle. Thanks to an extra set of eyelids, which are transparent and act like goggles, they can see equally well underwater or above. The moment they dive below the surface, automatic valves seal their nostrils and ears. And if they need to do some chewing while they're down there, they can close their lips behind their front teeth so they don't swallow any water.

If you've ever swum in cold water, you know how quickly it sucks the heat from your body. Beavers aren't bothered by even the chilliest water because of their specially designed swimwear. Closest to the skin, a layer of soft, thick underfur insulates like a cozy sweater. A layer of long, coarse guard hairs covers the underfur and acts

CASTOR FACT

Beaver fur is among the densest in the animal world, with up to about 150,000 hairs per square inch (23,000 hairs per square centimeter). By comparison, you probably have 170,000 to 200,000 hairs on your whole head.

like a wet suit. Even when beavers spend long stretches in the water, no moisture reaches their skin. That's because they have incredibly greasy fur, which sheds water instead of letting it soak in. The greasiness comes from a special oil produced by two glands located just inside the opening by the base of the tail.

Beavers spend a lot of time grooming themselves to keep their coats in prime condition. It's serious business, but it looks pretty funny. They use their front paws to rub the waterproofing oil through their fur, twisting and turning to get it all over their chubby bodies. They also scratch themselves with their hind feet, sometimes flopping over on one side to get at hard-to-reach areas. On the second toe of each back foot, they have a split nail that they use for untangling matted fur and removing dirt. It's as handy as carrying a comb in your back pocket.

When grooming themselves, beavers typically sit with their tail pointing forward.
REJEAN BEDARD/GETTY IMAGES

"THE BEST PET I EVER HAD"

BEAVER BACKERS

IN THE 1940s two of the most famous residents of Red Deer, Alberta, were a beaver called Mickey and the girl he lived with, Doris Forbes. They met in June 1939, when she was nine and he was about six weeks old. A neighbor found him on the sidewalk near her house one morning, with paralyzed hind legs and bloody gashes across his back. He still had his fuzzy baby-beaver fur coat and was so small Doris could hold him in one hand. No one expected the kit to recover, but within three days he was walking and his cuts soon healed.

Mickey remained with the Forbes family for the rest of his life. "He's the best pet I ever had and I love him with all my heart," Doris once said. Apparently Mickey felt the same way. When Doris went away for a few days, he got terribly upset, and the only thing that calmed him was hugging one of her sweaters.

Mickey slept in his kennel during the day and spent his nights playing with logs and boards in the garage. In the evenings he joined Doris and her parents in the house. If he was too dirty, Doris's mother tidied him up by running the vacuum cleaner over his coat before he came inside, much to his delight. Mickey loved building dams across the kitchen floor, using pieces of firewood

or the family's slippers. He also liked gnawing on wooden furniture until he was trained out of this habit. Doris fed Mickey branches, along with treats like apples, bananas and the occasional ice-cream cone. By the time he was two, he weighed nearly 70 pounds (32 kilograms).

Mickey lived for nine years and was a celebrity most of his life. Back then beavers were still rare in much of North America, and a pet beaver was truly unusual. Newspapers and magazines published articles about him, and the Canadian Broadcasting Corporation told his story on national radio. He even appeared in a Hollywood movie after a couple from Los Angeles filmed him during a visit. Altogether more than 20,000 people visited Mickey, and hundreds of others wrote letters to Doris about him.

Today they're still famous. If you go to Red Deer, you'll find a life-size bronze statue of the pair in a park near their former home. The story of Doris and Mickey continues to touch hearts, but attitudes have changed. Most people now understand that wild animals should live wild lives whenever possible. If you find an orphaned or injured beaver, take it to a wildlife rescue center, where it will receive expert care and be set free once it can survive on its own.

HUDSON'S BAY COMPANY ARCHIVES, ARCHIVES OF MANITOBA, A. KEEN PHOTOS OF DORIS FORBES AND MICKEY, CA. 1940

TEETH AND TAILS

The beaver's sturdy skull and jawbone and large front teeth are all made to stand up to a lifetime of chopping down trees, chewing through branches and peeling bark. Those front teeth never stop growing—a trait that all rodents share—but gnawing keeps them ground down to a suitable length. Gnawing also keeps these essential tools in good working order. That's because the front of each incisor is covered with hard, iron-rich orange enamel, while the rest of the tooth is made of softer, white dentin. With every bite, the enamel of the lower teeth shaves away some of the dentin on the upper teeth, creating a chisel-sharp edge.

Beavers use their front teeth for cutting and peeling, and their cheek teeth for grinding.
GRAFXART8888/GETTY IMAGES

The beaver's tail is one of the most distinctive and versatile parts of its anatomy. This flat, paddle-shaped appendage is covered with leathery scales and controlled by numerous muscles and tendons. Beavers use their tails as a rudder for steering when swimming and diving, as a prop to keep themselves stable when felling trees and as a pantry for storing fat reserves. Inside the tail, a network of blood vessels helps beavers stay warm in winter and cool in summer.

Last but not least, beaver tails are also important communication devices.

Beavers move through the water by kicking their webbed hind feet and steering with their tails. Their top swimming speed is about 5 miles (8 kilometers) an hour.
BARBARAAAA/GETTY IMAGES

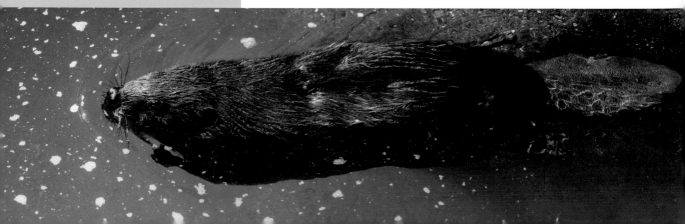

CASTORID COMMUNICATIONS

SMACK! The explosive sound of a beaver's tail striking the water is dramatic and unforgettable. For me it's the sound of wilderness—of a misty lake at dawn or a wide, lazy river reflecting sunset colors. But these days you could as easily hear that distinctive whack in the middle of a city.

Beavers slap their tails to alert family members to sudden danger, just as you would shout out a warning. As the tail slapper broadcasts this noisy alarm, it often dives out of sight, throwing up a fountain of water. Any beaver within hearing distance usually reacts immediately. If it's on land, it scurries to the water and plunges in. If it's already swimming, it dives beneath the surface and may head for the safety of the lodge. Responders often add their own tail slaps to reinforce the original message.

Adults do more tail slapping than younger beavers do, and their warnings are taken more seriously. Family members pay close attention when the danger signal comes from a parent, especially the mother. And they often ignore the tail slaps of kits and juveniles, who tend to send out more false alarms. Beavers can identify the source of the slap because a youngster's smaller, narrower tail doesn't smack down as loudly as a full-sized adult tail.

Beavers also communicate vocally. If you sit quietly near a lodge and listen carefully, you may hear whines, grunts or other sounds of conversation. In spring and early summer, soft mewing from within the lodge will tell you there are hungry kits inside, begging for food. Adult vocalizations include hissing and growling—signs that the beaver is angry, agitated or afraid.

Although beavers have mediocre eyesight, that's not a problem. They mostly conduct their business in the dark of night and spend their days resting inside their lightless lodges. Sharp ears and a keen sense of smell make up for what they lack in vision. Beavers use their noses constantly—to sniff out their favorite foods, to detect lurking predators, to identify other beavers and to inspect territorial boundaries.

Inside a beaver lodge in Grand Teton National Park, an adult grooms itself while keeping an eye on the kits.
NATIONAL GEOGRAPHIC IMAGE COLLECTION / ALAMY STOCK PHOTO

TERRITORIAL MARKING AND A CURE FOR HEADACHES

If you walk along the edge of a pond or river that's home to beavers, you may come across odd-looking piles of mud. They can be as small as a Frisbee or as big as a car tire. They also have a unique smell, though you may not detect it unless you get down on your knees and sniff the mud. These mud piles, known as scent mounds, mark a beaver family's territory. They're like advertising billboards, but instead of using flashing lights and bright colors to send out a message, they use invisible, nose-tingling chemicals.

To make a scent mound, a beaver dredges up soft mud from underwater and plops it onto the shore. Once it's satisfied with the size of the pile, the beaver squats over it and squirts a stinky, yellowish-brown substance called *castoreum* onto it. Like a graffiti artist's tag, a shot of castoreum is a unique personal signature that can be "read" by the nose of any passing beaver. By building and tagging mud mounds, or sometimes just twists of grass, beavers claim ownership of their territory and tell strangers to get lost.

The importance of castoreum to beavers is obvious, but this substance is also very valuable in the human world. For centuries castoreum has been a key component in expensive perfumes. To my nose, it smells like a blend of tar and leather, with floral undertones—not horrible, but not exactly something I'd want to splash on my skin before going to a party. Yet somehow mixing castoreum with other perfume ingredients produces lovely scents.

In ancient times, physicians used castoreum in remedies for numerous ailments, including headaches, toothaches, deafness, epilepsy, liver tumors and madness.

This beaver-scent mound by the Sammamish River in Washington State is an impressive 1.5 feet (0.5 meters) tall.
JENNIFER VANDERHOOF

Castoreum, a smelly substance produced by beavers, is the surprising secret ingredient in some perfumes.
VISOOT UTHAIRAM/GETTY IMAGES

Although you won't find those medicines in your local drugstore, modern-day chemistry tells us that the ancient healers had the right idea. We now know that castoreum contains salicylic acid, the active ingredient in the pain-killer aspirin, and that the salicylic acid in castoreum comes from the bark of the beaver's preferred food trees—willows, aspens and poplars. You could say that beavers helped invent a cure for headaches.

KITS HAVE IT EASY

Beavers are typically born in May or June. There are usually two to four kits in a litter, though there can be just one or as many as nine. A newborn beaver is about the size and weight of a pound (454 grams) of butter and looks like a miniature version of its parents. At first kits stay cuddled up in the lodge and get all their nutrition from their mother's milk. By the time they're a month old, they've mostly switched to the adult menu.

A kit and an older family member nibble on opposite ends of a branch. Sharing comes naturally to beavers.
RUSTY COHN

Fuzzy-furred baby beavers score
10 out of 10 on the cuteness scale.
LITTLE_THINGS/GETTY IMAGES

The kits spend their first summer exploring, learning and playing. They can swim and dive within a few days of being born, but they can't spend a long time in the water until they get their fur well waterproofed, which takes several weeks. During early trips out of the lodge, they often hitch rides on their parents' backs. As they become stronger swimmers, they get more independent but still stick close to their parents and older siblings. They watch their elders working on dams and felling trees and then start to practice these skills themselves.

GROWING UP AND MOVING ON

Beavers continue to live with their parents through their second and sometimes their third year. At this point they're called juveniles. Like many human teenagers, juvenile beavers have to do chores. They fell trees and work on building *food caches*. They assist with dam and lodge

Like human kids, young beavers enjoy riding on their parents' backs.
JEFF MOLLMAN

During their first excursions out of the lodge, beaver kits stick close to their parents and older siblings for protection and guidance. RUSTY COHN

repairs and maintenance. They help keep the lodge tidy by clearing out soiled bedding. And when they're out and about, they provide extra ears and eyes to detect danger and extra tails to slap out warnings.

It's a good thing beaver families get along so well, because they spend a lot of time in close quarters, especially in winter. During the coldest months they rarely leave home. The lodge is also the family's main daytime hangout during the rest of the year. Webcams installed inside lodges often show the inhabitants eating side by side, grooming each other or cozying up together as they sleep.

Eventually juveniles are ready to leave home and start their own families. This usually happens around the time a new litter of kits arrives in the spring. Heading off in various directions, the juveniles wander about, searching for a place of their own and a mate to share it with.

This transition period is filled with hazards, and many juveniles don't survive. They're still inexperienced, they're traveling through unfamiliar terrain and usually sleeping in temporary bank dens, and they're on their own, with no one to look out for them. They must be constantly on guard, dodging predators, watching for vehicles and avoiding traps. They also have to steer clear of other beavers' homes. Beavers are highly territorial animals and

This beaver made it across the road without getting hit. Many others aren't so lucky.
DEVON OPDENDRIES/GETTY IMAGES

will chase off or attack trespassers. Brawls often leave the combatants with permanent scars and nicked or notched tails, and sometimes such fights even end in death.

Beavers that make it past all those dangers and reach adulthood have a good chance of living for many more years. Once they find a partner and settle down, they will stay with that mate for life and produce a new litter of kits each spring. The typical beaver life-span in the wild is about 10 years, although the hardiest individuals may live twice as long.

A yellow water-lily flower makes a satisfying mouthful for a beaver as it floats among the lily pads.
JENNIFER VANDERHOOF

TREE BARK, POOP AND OTHER TASTY SNACKS

Beavers are strict vegetarians, and their most important food is cambium, the sugary inner bark of trees and shrubs. They prefer leafy deciduous trees, such as aspen, willow, alder and maple, and turn up their noses at pine, spruce, fir and other conifers unless they're the only trees around.

Trees and shrubs also provide many of the other items on the beaver grocery list, from twigs, buds and leaves to fruits and nuts. When fresh greenery is available, beavers happily chow down on grasses, ferns, flowering plants and everything in between.

In many areas, water lilies are a favorite beaver food. The animals munch on the fat blossoms. They roll up the leaves and eat them like burritos. And they dive down to the bottom of ponds to dig up the lilies' thick underground stems, called *tubers*.

Cattails are also popular fare. When beavers dine on these delicacies, they grasp the cattail stalk with their

CASTOR FACT

Beavers fed by a caretaker in Colorado each ate about a ton (907 kilograms) of aspen per year.

Beavers eat all kinds of leafy and shrubby plants. ANN CAMERON SIEGAL

Beavers usually deposit their second-pass droppings in water. Whether the pellets sink to the bottom or float depends on what kind of plants the beaver had been eating. Either way, they are rarely seen. PAUL STAROSTA/GETTY IMAGES

two front paws and turn it as they nibble, much like you probably tackle corn on the cob.

Bark contains a lot of *cellulose*, the same stuff that the pages of this book are made from. As you can imagine, cellulose is hard to digest. Specialized microbes that live in beavers' guts help break down the cellulose, but for those microbes to do their job properly, beavers have to eat everything twice. They do this by consuming their own poop!

The first time a beaver defecates after a meal, its feces are soft and dark. It eats those droppings, which sounds disgusting but is actually very practical. Another round of digestion allows beavers to extract more *nutrients* from their food. The small, hard pellets that come out after the second pass have the consistency—and the nutritional value—of packed sawdust.

Autumn is a busy time for beavers as they work hard to stock up on food for the winter.
STAN TEKIELA AUTHOR / NATURALIST / WILDLIFE PHOTOGRAPHER/GETTY IMAGES

With winter approaching, the beavers living in this New Jersey pond have built a food cache next to their lodge. When the pond freezes over, they will reach the stored food by swimming under the ice. CHUCK GARRETT

WINTER DINING

In winter, beavers have fewer food choices. Many plants die back, and snow buries others, though that doesn't stop beavers from getting out and foraging. They'll plow through snow or waddle on top of it to get to trees and shrubs that are still exposed. But if they live in a place where the water freezes and they can't get to land, they need a different strategy.

Beavers don't mind if their pond freezes over at the surface as long as there's enough water below the ice for them to come and go from their lodge through the underwater doorways. If a pond isn't naturally deep enough to keep from freezing right to the bottom, they use their dam-construction skills to raise the water level. As winter approaches, beaver families prepare by building food caches—huge piles of branches anchored to the bottom of the pond near their lodge. Sometimes beavers also stash water-lily tubers in their caches.

A food cache is like a well-stocked refrigerator. Throughout the winter, beavers swim out under the ice whenever they're hungry and pull branches from their caches. They take these provisions back to the lodge and eat in comfort, and later they chuck the peeled sticks back into the pond. Come spring, those sticks will be useful for dam repairs.

Standing in an icy puddle on a frozen pond looks uncomfortable, but this beaver isn't complaining. Special networks of blood vessels inside its tail and hind feet keep the cold from traveling through its body.
ANN CAMERON SIEGAL

Glynnis Hood (in the red jacket) and Gillian Larsen have climbed onto this beaver lodge to check whether it's occupied. If they see frost crystals around the rooftop vents, they'll know that beavers are living inside the lodge. KAYLEIGH BARTLEY

BEAVERS LIVE IN some of the coldest parts of North America, but unlike many northern animals, they don't hibernate or migrate. Instead they rely on a wide range of other strategies to survive the season of snow and ice.

As winter approaches, beavers' bodies change to prepare for cold weather and lean times. Their fur gets thicker to provide more insulation, and they pack on extra body fat for both warmth and stored energy. Their most unusual winter survival trick is turning their tail into an energy stash. A beaver can store so much fat in its tail over the summer that it doubles in size. As the beaver draws on this reserve during the winter, the tail flattens out again.

Beavers begin getting ready for winter in late summer and carry on through the fall. Adults and juveniles work hard during this time, building food caches, ensuring their dams are in good condition and adding mud, sticks and vegetation to the outside of their lodge. When this mud freezes, it's as hard as concrete. It keeps predators from breaking in, even though ice may create a bridge that allows them to walk right up to the beavers' home.

The lodge's thick walls also keep the interior temperature from dipping below freezing, and snow adds extra insulation. Inside, family members snuggle together to share their body heat. In the constant darkness, all their communication is by touch, sound and smell. Those same senses also tell them when they have company. Glynnis Hood, a biologist who lives in Alberta and studies beavers, describes beaver lodges in winter as "little hotels." Muskrats often move in, and voles may come calling. The beavers don't seem to mind. After all, extra bodies offer extra warmth.

On windless winter days, you might see what looks like smoke rising from a snow-covered beaver lodge. That's the residents' steamy breath escaping through the rooftop ventilation holes and condensing in the cold outside air. If the air is cold enough and still enough, the steam will crystallize into huge frost formations, like ghostly globes made out of icy feathers. Glynnis likes to crawl up onto beaver lodges in winter to examine the frost formations.

If you follow her example and climb to the top of a lodge, be prepared to be slammed by what Glynnis calls "the aroma of winter beavers" when you get close to the vent. Sometimes the smell is so powerful that you'll get a whiff of it before you even reach the lodge. Things get rather stinky when you're living in close quarters with little ventilation.

When the winter freeze begins, beavers sometimes keep their swimming routes open by butting the ice from below with their heads to break it or by chewing at it. In spring they may do the same to speed the thaw. But during the coldest months, they're sealed off from the outside world, confined to their lodge and the water beneath the ice. Air trapped in their fur helps insulate their bodies when they venture out into the frigid pond. As they swim, the water squeezes the air from their coats and bubbles stream out behind them. If you brush the snow off the ice near a beaver lodge, you might see a trail of white, coin-sized circles—frozen air bubbles that offer a glimpse into the beavers' secret winter existence.

As long as some water remains unfrozen, beavers can still reach the world above the ice. The residents of this lodge soon will be locked in for the winter.
MATTHEW_MILLER/GETTY IMAGES

Beavers are unintentional water-lily farmers. When they eat the seed pods, the seeds pass through their guts undamaged. And when they dredge up mud for building, they create good growing sites for those seeds.
REJEAN BEDARD/GETTY IMAGES

2
HABITAT MAKERS AND COMMUNITY CREATORS

TIIIM-BER!!

To fell a tree, a beaver stands with its front paws braced against the trunk and its tail extended for balance. Then it tilts its head and starts gnawing. As the beaver works, it turns its head from side to side and shuffles this way and that, circling the tree and chomping deeper and deeper into the trunk. When there's no longer enough wood left to support the weight of the trunk and branches above the cutting zone, the tree crashes to the ground.

If you think tree felling sounds dangerous, you're right. Beavers seldom get killed on the job, but accidents do happen. Sometimes a tree keels over so suddenly that the tree cutter gets whacked before it can scurry out of the way. More often, fatalities happen when a beaver has chewed deep into a large tree and the upper part of the trunk suddenly slips down onto the lower part, crushing the unlucky victim's head. Fortunately, those incidents are rare. That's partly because young beavers learn the tricks of the trade by observing or working alongside their parents and older siblings.

A motion-activated infrared trail camera can reveal what happens under the cover of darkness. These beavers worked on this tree for many nights, then left it teetering on what little trunk remained. The wind blew it over a couple of weeks later.
DOUG KNUTSON, WINDSWEPT PRODUCTIONS

Usually beavers target fairly small trees, because they can be felled quickly and they have thinner, more digestible bark. A beaver can cut down one medium-sized tree or several smaller ones in a single night. Felling a big tree can take weeks of nightly gnawing sessions, but the payoff is a wealth of wood. The largest beaver-cut stump on record measured three and a half feet (just over one meter) across. To hug a tree that massive, you'd need to join hands with at least two friends.

Adult beavers mostly work alone when felling trees. Occasionally two will work on one tree at the same time. Family members also sometimes take turns chiseling away at a larger tree. In the end, they all benefit from the shared labor.

Colorful new growth sprouts from a beaver-cut aspen stump.
FRANCES BACKHOUSE

CASTOR FACT

When beavers cut down aspens, new shoots quickly sprout up from the stumps. These young trees protect themselves against further attacks by producing high concentrations of bad-tasting chemicals in their bark. The bark of older aspens contains the same defensive chemicals, but in smaller doses.

When felling a tree, beavers try to control the direction it will drop. They instinctively make strategic decisions about the position and order of the cuts. Most of the time they get it right.
LYNN_BYSTROM/GETTY IMAGES

Once beavers have brought down a tree, there's still lots of work to do. They may take time to gnaw off some of the bark and nibble a few twigs and leaves, but mainly they focus on lopping off the branches and cutting the trunk into shorter sections so they can drag everything to the shore and float it out into the water.

The shorter the distance beavers have to haul their booty overland the better, so when they cut down a tree, they want it to topple toward the shoreline. Amazingly, they're smart enough to ensure that this usually happens. Nearly three-quarters of all large trees cut down by beavers fall in the direction of the water.

It takes patience and persistence to chew through the trunk of a large tree like this cottonwood. TROY HARRISON/GETTY IMAGES

MASTER BUILDERS AT WORK

Beavers build dams to make ponds and spread water out across the land. Having lots of water around is important to them for a few reasons. It provides safe travel routes for getting to and from onshore work sites. It makes their lodges more secure. And as long as it's deep enough, it allows them to survive freezing winters, because they can swim out under the ice and get food from their caches. Because dams are so useful, beavers often build a series of them along a stream or river, creating a chain of ponds like beads on a string.

While all beaver dams have the same basic design, local conditions influence the details of the structure—how high and wide it is, how straight or curved, and what

Whether working or playing, beavers are safer in the water than on land.
TROY HARRISON/GETTY IMAGES

Beavers building a dam on Napa Creek in California add round river rocks for extra strength. RUSTY COHN

it's made of. Wood is always the first choice, but if trees are in short supply, beavers will use whatever's available. Their more unconventional construction materials include corn cobs, corn stalks, boulders and all kinds of items discarded by humans, from plastic buckets to car tires. One of the weirdest items ever found in a beaver dam was an artificial leg. Another dam had an old steel beaver trap wedged in between the sticks and logs, where it was guaranteed to do no more harm.

Beavers typically begin dam construction by ramming leafy branches, cut ends down, into the bottom and banks of a stream and anchoring them with mud and stones. This creates the base. Then they build upward, piling on more branches and shoving them together so they become tightly interlocked. As the dam grows higher, the engineers close up any gaps and seal the top and sides with mud, which is sometimes mixed with grass and leaves.

Long ago many people believed that beavers used their tails like wheelbarrows to haul mud when building dams or lodges and then as trowels to slap the mud onto these structures. Not true! Beavers actually scoop up the mud with their front paws and carry it clutched against their chests. Sometimes they use a one-arm hold and hump along on their other three limbs. If they need both arms to hold a load, they rise up on their hind legs and toddle. Beavers sometimes also carry stones or short sticks this way, using either the one- or two-arm technique. When they need to transport longer branches or logs, they grasp them near the cut end with their powerful jaws and drag them across the ground or tow them through the water.

On an autumn evening in Alaska, a beaver waddles up the side of its lodge clasping an armload of mud to its chest.
PAUL SOUDERS/GETTY IMAGES

BEAVER TALES
DAMS, FROM MASSIVE TO MINI

Jean Thie points to the exceptional feat of beaver engineering that he discovered in 2007. The wetland created by the dam is shown in purple on a map Thie produced using Bing Maps. The second screen displays a Google Earth image of North America, where Jean has mapped several thousand beaver dams. MARJOLIJN THIE

Seen from the air, Wood Buffalo National Park's famously long beaver dam is easy to spot. It's the meandering line that separates the blue water and bright green wetland vegetation on the right from the dark green forest on the left. PARKS CANADA/WOOD BUFFALO NATIONAL PARK

JEAN THIE ENJOYS exploring the world through computer programs such as Google Earth and NASA WorldWind. Jean is a landscape ecologist who has a special interest in beavers. As he spins the globe with a click of his mouse, zooming in and out, he looks for dams and lodges to see where beavers are active.

In 2007, while virtually "flying" over Wood Buffalo National Park in northern Alberta, Jean spotted a beaver dam that was much longer than any others he'd ever seen. He measured it with

the Google Earth measuring tool and found it was 2,790 feet (850 meters) long—almost the length of 30 NBA basketball courts laid end to end.

Using WorldWind imagery and aerial photos, Jean figured out that beavers started building this super dam in the early 1980s. It's the longest beaver dam known to exist anywhere in the world now, but probably not the longest ever. David Thompson was a surveyor and mapmaker who traveled across North America in the late 1700s and early 1800s. He once encountered a beaver dam that was 1 mile

The pool behind this dam in the Skagit River Delta isn't much bigger than a bathtub, but it provides important habitat for young salmon and other small fish.
FRANCES BACKHOUSE

(1.6 kilometers) long and wide enough for two horses to walk across it side by side!

In contrast, the world's shortest beaver dams average about 6 feet (1.8 meters) in length. These mini dams are found along the narrow channels that flow through the tidal marshes of the Skagit River Delta in Washington State. Some of them are as little as 12 inches (30 centimeters) long.

The height of beaver dams is less variable than the length. Exceptionally tall dams can reach heights of up to 15 feet (4.6 meters), but most top out at around 10 feet (3 meters). That's because the taller a dam is, the stronger it has to be to hold back the water pushing against it. The world's shortest beaver dam might be one in the Skagit River Delta that measured a mere 8 inches (20 centimeters) high.

As for the world's longest dam, it's only a few feet tall. The land in that part of Wood Buffalo National Park is so flat that the beavers need only a low barrier to create a suitable pond.

NO LEAKS ALLOWED

Beavers have a reputation for busyness, and one of the tasks that keeps them busiest is dam maintenance. They conduct frequent dam patrols, checking for leaks as they swim past. If necessary, they climb onto the dam for closer assessment. When repairs are required, they make them promptly. Adults do most of the dam inspections and maintenance. Usually they work alone, but if there's a major breach, family members will join forces to fix it as quickly as possible.

Beavers generally do their dam patrols at night, so they're more likely to hear water trickling over or through a dam than see it. The importance of listening for leaks makes beavers extremely sensitive to the sound of running water and fanatical about trying to block it, no matter the source. People who bring beavers into their homes as pets or rescue animals soon learn that the sound of a toilet flushing or a bathtub filling is likely to provoke a frenzy of attempted dam repair, using towels or anything else that's handy.

When beavers have enough water, they may let some escape over the top of a dam. If they need their pond to be deeper or bigger, they add material on the upstream side of the dam to raise its height.
TROY HARRISON/GETTY IMAGES

Beaver lodges and dams are built on strong underwater foundations. Construction begins with anchoring pieces of cut wood to the bottom of the pond or stream.
ASTRID860/GETTY IMAGES

LODGE LOGISTICS

Like dams, freestanding beaver lodges are built from the bottom up. The beavers start by gathering branches and sections of tree trunk, floating them out into a pond or shallow lake and heaping them on the bottom. All the initial construction work takes place underwater. Each time the beavers dive down, they add more material, cramming thinner sticks in between bulkier logs and filling the gaps with mud and debris. Later, when the mound reaches the surface of the water, they clamber up on top to deposit their freight.

Once the tightly packed pile extends high enough above the water, the builders swim down to the base and tackle the interior design in a way that no other animal,

CASTOR FACT

Beavers can hold their breath underwater for as long as 15 minutes, but they usually come up for air sooner than that.

The peaks of the Teton Range tower over this serene beaver pond in Wyoming.
ZEN RIAL/GETTY IMAGES

including humans, possibly could. They gnaw at the woody mass until they've chewed their way up and into the center, where they carve out their living quarters. Imagine constructing your bedroom by chomping through a truckload of two-by-fours!

The final step is to plaster the exterior of the lodge with mud, which dries into a hard shell that protects and insulates. The beavers leave a few small ventilation holes in the roof for air flow, but there are no windows, so it's completely dark inside.

A lodge can be as small as a garden shed or as big as a two-car garage. Beavers can build even a large lodge surprisingly quickly, going from start to finish in just a few nights. And a well-built lodge can last for decades.

Beaver lodges get bigger over time as their owners add more branches and mud to the outside. Fall is prime time for home renovations.
ENRIQUE AGUIRRE AVES/GETTY IMAGES

BEAVER BACKERS

IF YOUR IDEA of a good time includes camping, bushwhacking, wading in streams and wallowing in mud, you would love being part of Montana's Citizen Science Beaver Assessment Program. Every summer, crews of Montana Conservation Corps (MCC) youth volunteers head out to Lolo National Forest near Missoula to gather data for the United States Forest Service and a conservation organization called the Clark Fork Coalition.

Each MCC youth crew spends six days in the field. Led by two counselors, they learn about beavers, search for signs of beaver activity and study streams to see if they would be good places for beavers to live in the future. Much of the work happens right in the streams they're investigating, so everyone spends a lot of time wearing rubber chest waders.

Garrett Goulstone got involved in this **citizen science** project in 2019, when he was 12 years old. "I liked wading in the streams," he says. "Collecting data was fun too."

Whenever they came to a data-collection point, he and his five fellow crew members pulled clipboards,

Members of a Montana Conservation Corps youth crew make their way up a stream while assessing beaver habitat in Lolo National Forest. BONITA PERNOT, CLARK FORK COALITION

cameras, tape measures, depth sticks and other equipment out of their backpacks. Then they fanned out to find the information needed to rate the site's beaver-habitat potential. Garrett's favorite job was measuring the stream gradient (or slope), using an instrument called a *clinometer*. The crew also measured the width of the stream and the depth of the places where it formed pools. They made notes about whether the streambed was covered with sand, gravel or cobblestones and evaluated bank erosion. And they counted the beaver-food trees and shrubs growing along that section of the stream.

Garrett and the other 35 middle schoolers who participated in this program in 2019 surveyed 14.5 miles (23 kilometers) of stream. Garrett's group didn't see any beavers, but they did get a chance to splash around in some unoccupied beaver ponds.

"They were really muddy at the bottom, and I got stuck a few times," Garrett recalls with a laugh. All in a day's work for a dedicated beaver researcher.

Garrett Goulstone, all packed and ready for adventure. CATHERINE OFF

A canal made by beavers winds through boggy terrain in Ontario's Algonquin Provincial Park.
FRANCES BACKHOUSE

DIG THIS

The beaver's least-known engineering skill is *canal* construction. If the soil is soft enough, beavers often dig these channels out from the edges of their pond to gain better access to trees. It's much safer for them to swim from place to place than to walk. It's also easier for them to move materials by water than by land.

Many beaver canals look like insignificant ditches and are hidden by overhanging vegetation. The first time I noticed them was while hiking with biologist Glynnis Hood near her home in the Beaver Hills in central Alberta. As she showed me, the beavers that live in this area are enthusiastic channel diggers. Some of their waterways are more than 200 yards (183 meters) long, 3 feet (1 meter) wide and 3 feet (1 meter) deep. On several occasions Glynnis has checked their depth the hard way—by accidentally falling into them! Incredibly, beavers excavate these extensive canal systems one muddy pawful at a time.

Beavers also dig channels in pond bottoms. These underwater trenches provide extra depth for swimming when the pond freezes over in winter or the water level drops in summer.

BEAVERS ON BULLDOZERS

Besides controlling the flow of water, beaver dams can affect the shape of the land. All flowing water erodes the land it travels along, grinding rocks and dirt into fine sediment (or silt) that it carries downstream. When a river or creek is slowed by a beaver dam, the sediment settles to the bottom behind the dam. Sometimes there's a little, and sometimes there's a lot. A team of scientists working in Quebec calculated that one small beaver dam could trap enough sediment to fill 1,700 dump trucks!

Over time ponds can fill right up with silt, forcing the beavers to leave and find a new home. As plants take root, the old pond turns into a wet, grassy *beaver meadow*. Eventually trees and shrubs sprout up. When this growth

Generations of beavers have created this wide, flat beaver meadow, high in the Rocky Mountains in Colorado.
EMILY FAIRFAX

is big enough, beavers will return, dam the creek and start the process all over again. It can take decades, or even centuries, for this beaver cycle to come full circle.

Over hundreds or thousands of years, repeated dam building and pond filling can change the way the land looks. Landscape changes can also happen so quickly that it's as if the beavers were driving around on bulldozers. For instance, major flooding can wash a large amount of sediment from a beaver pond out onto the surrounding land. Humans may not like the results, but plants such as willows will quickly take advantage of these new growing spaces.

KEYSTONE CONNECTIONS

Beavers belong to an exclusive club of animals called keystone species. In a stone arch, the keystone is a wedge-shaped block that sits at the top of the structure and locks all the other pieces into place. If the keystone is pulled out, the arch collapses—just like a Jenga tower crashes down if you remove a key block. In nature, a keystone species plays a special role in its community, supporting other species and helping to keep the whole *ecosystem*

Stonemasons long ago learned how to build arches from wedge-shaped stones. The keystone at the top is set in place last and supports the rest of the stones. This ancient arch is in Cyprus.
SARAH BATES

Wetlands cover only a small percentage of the earth's surface but are among the world's most valuable ecosystems. They store and purify water and provide essential habitat for many plants and animals.
FRANCES BACKHOUSE

functioning properly. If a keystone species is removed, the community it supports is weakened and may break down completely.

Beavers play their keystone role by creating wetlands—including ponds, marshes and swamps—that provide essential *habitat* for many animals and plants. Wetlands are among the world's most biologically productive ecosystems, right up there with rainforests and coral reefs. In other words, wetlands are home to a greater variety and abundance of plants and animals than most other ecosystems. And because wetlands are one of the world's most threatened habitats, many of the plants and animals that live in them are in danger of becoming extinct. In North America, we have beavers to thank for developing and maintaining much of our wetland habitat.

When you visit a beaver pond, it's easy to see the richness of life that exists there. The first thing you might

Snapping turtles like to live in places with slow-moving water, a soft muddy or sandy bottom and lots of aquatic plants. Beaver ponds are ideal.
FRANCES BACKHOUSE

Beavers and moose are often neighbors. Moose feast on aquatic plants in summer, and on hot days they spend hours in the water, trying to stay cool.
FRANCES BACKHOUSE

This young beaver has a lifetime of habitat creation ahead of it.
TERRYFIC3D/GETTY IMAGES

observe is how lush the surrounding vegetation is. That's because water from the pond is seeping out into the ground around it, and the thirsty plants are drinking it up. Plant eaters like deer and voles love to browse on the well-watered shoreline greenery. Moose, on the other hand, prefer to wade in deep to feast on water lilies and other aquatic plants.

Dip a net into the water and you'll discover that it's teeming with *plankton* and insects. These small creatures, some so tiny that you need a microscope to see them, are at the center of the beaver-pond food web. Fish and tadpoles gobble them down and are eaten in turn by herons, king-fishers, minks, raccoons and other predators. As for those mosquitoes that are buzzing around your ears, they'll get snapped up by dragonflies, frogs, swallows and bats.

Beavers also provide living space and housing for other community members. Beaver ponds and canals offer a wide range of real estate options for fish, amphibians (frogs, toads and salamanders), turtles and semi-aquatic mammals such as muskrats and otters. Trees killed by beaver flooding are equally useful. Woodpeckers drill into

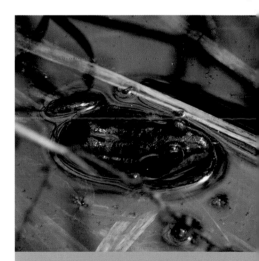

Beavers provide important habitat for amphibians, like this green frog. Despite their name, green frogs can be green, brown, bronze or a combination of these colors.
FRANCES BACKHOUSE

A viewing platform helps wetland visitors get closer to the action. The platform to the left of this pond offers an excellent view of the beaver lodge. SCHROPTSCHOP/GETTY IMAGES

the dying and dead trees to make their nest holes. Once they move on, other birds, such as swallows, claim these spaces. For wood ducks and other cavity-nesting ducks like buffleheads, goldeneyes and mergansers, these old nest holes in trees next to beaver ponds are ideal homes. When their ducklings are ready to leave the nest, they can launch straight out the front door of their high-rise residence and drop into the water.

The list of species that depend on beavers and their engineering work varies from place to place. A beaver pond in Arizona hosts different plants and animals than one in the Northwest Territories, for example. But no matter where they're found, beaver habitats are always lively places with a large cast of characters.

Like beavers, black-crowned night-herons are most active between dusk and dawn. Could this one be thanking the beaver for providing the wetland habitat it needs for nesting and feeding?
RUSTY COHN

Beaverlodge's gigantic beaver sculpture is 18 feet (5.5 meters) long and weighs 1,500 pounds (680 kilograms). That's not including the log it sits on, which doubles the weight. Altogether the sculpture stands 15 feet (4.5 meters) high.

3
FROM SLAUGHTER TO SALVATION

BEAVERLAND

If you live in Canada or any US state other than Hawaii, there's probably some sort of beaver landmark near your home. But don't just take my word for it. Take a look at a map.

My local beaver landmark is Beaver Lake, or, I should say, *one* of the Beaver Lakes. There are at least 200 of them in North America. There are also many other lakes named for beavers, including Beaverhouse, Beaverflood, Beaverjack, Beavertrap, Beaverhide, Beaver Claw, Beaverpaw, Beaverleg, Beaverhead, Beavertail, Beavertooth and Beaverkit. Whew! That's a lot of beavers. And the lakes are only the beginning.

All kinds of other geographical features also pay tribute to beavers—for example, Beaver Creek, Beaver Canyon, Beaver Glacier, Beaver Bluffs, Beaver Flats and Beaver City. Some of the more unusual names I've come across include Beaver Bottom, Beaver Steady, Beaver Lick and Beaver Medicine Falls. In Alberta there's a town called Beaverlodge, which is home to the world's largest beaver sculpture.

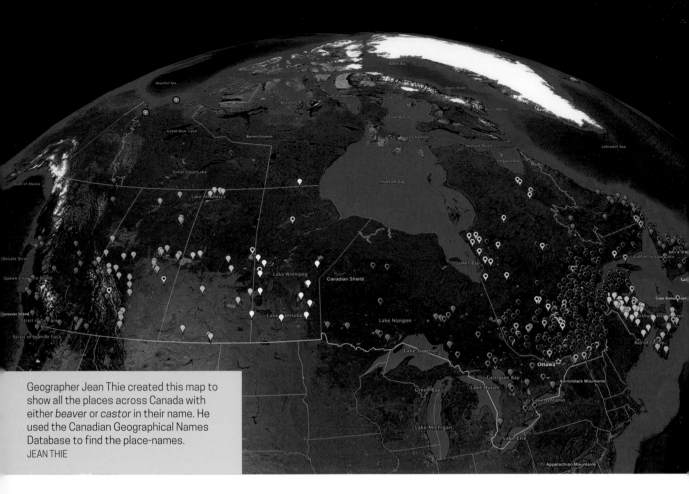

Geographer Jean Thie created this map to show all the places across Canada with either *beaver* or *castor* in their name. He used the Canadian Geographical Names Database to find the place-names.
JEAN THIE

CASTOR FACT

The Vuntut Gwich'in, who live in the Yukon, have many words for beavers. The all-purpose word is *tsèe*. If you want to be more specific, you can say *neezhìi* (one-year-old beaver), *ch'aachii* (two-year-old beaver), *ch'edoovii* (three-year-old beaver) or *ch'ichoo* (a very large beaver). A female beaver is *tsèe tr'ik*, and a male is *tsèe dinjii*.

Beaver place-names also show up in other languages. Amik Lake? In Anishinaabemowin, the language of the Anishinaabe peoples, *amik* means "beaver." Amisk Lake? Now we're in Cree territory. Or how about Castorville, Bayou Castor, Lac du Castor Solitaire, Prairie du Castor, Castor Point and Castor Plunge? If you speak French or Spanish, you may know that the word for beaver in both of those languages is *castor*.

Altogether there are more than 2,000 places named for beavers on this continent. They're scattered across every province, territory and state. No other animal has such a prominent presence on the North American map. That tells us just how common and widespread beavers once were.

However, for a while it looked like beavers would be wiped right off the map. If that had happened, we would have been left with only those place-names to remember them by.

BROWN GOLD

The original human inhabitants of this continent developed their relationship with beavers over tens of thousands of years. This relationship was based on existing in balance with all living and nonliving things and taking only what they needed. When Europeans arrived, they came with a different worldview, and as they spread out across North America they did many things that upset the balance of nature and harmed the environment. Beavers were one of the casualties.

In the 1500s crews from France, Spain, Portugal and England started crossing the ocean to catch cod and whales off the east coast of North America. When they went ashore, some of them did a little trading with the people who lived along the coast, such as the Mi'kmaq. The seafarers exchanged knives and other items for animal pelts, then sold the pelts when they returned home. Once the European fur buyers realized how abundant beavers were in North America, casual trading turned into big business.

Europe had its own beavers, but *Castor fiber* was not doing well. A couple of centuries earlier, European hatters had discovered that felted beaver fur is a fantastic hat-making material. The short hairs that make up the soft underfur are covered with microscopic scales, and each scale is tipped with an exceptionally long barb, like a fishhook. During the felting process, the barbs grab each other and lock together, creating a strong, hard-wearing, water-repellent fabric.

This gentleman's top hat was made from felted beaver fur around 1880.
NANCY PEARSON

CASTOR FACT
How to Make a Beaver Hat

1.
Pluck the long guard hairs from the pelt and discard them.

2.
Shave off the underfur and process it to remove tangles and dirt, then fluff it into loose bundles.

3.
Use heat, pressure and moisture to condense the bundles into thick sheets.

4.
Shape the sheets into cones that look like large dunce caps.

5.
Dump the cones into a huge kettle filled with a hot acidic solution and stir them around.

6.
Once the cones have shrunk to about half their original size, fish them out and stretch them over hat-shaped wooden blocks. Remove when dry.

7.
Refine the shape of each hat and finish it off with lining and trim.

A 19th-century fur trader stands in a room filled with bundled and loose pelts of beavers, foxes, minks and other animals. This photo was taken at Fort Chipewyan, an Alberta town named after the area's original people—the Chipewyan or Denésuliné.
UNKNOWN PHOTOGRAPHER/LIBRARY AND ARCHIVES CANADA/ERNEST BROWN FONDS/E011303100-012_S1

As demand for felted beaver-fur hats soared, beaver numbers plummeted. It took two to three beaver pelts to make a single top hat, and even more for some other hat styles. By the time Europeans reached North America, they had nearly driven the Eurasian beaver to extinction and the hatters were running out of beaver fur. Those desperate hatters were thrilled when cod fishermen and whalers showed up with beaver pelts from what they called "the New World." Bring us as many as you can, they said, and we'll pay you handsomely. Soon ships were sailing to North America just to load up with furs, especially the prized beaver furs.

Although the transatlantic fur trade started on the east coast of North America, it grew to cover the whole continent. The traders were relentless in their pursuit of beavers and kept pushing farther west, north and south, eradicating beavers as they went. Everyone was scrambling to gather as much "brown gold" as they could before someone else got it.

FUR-TRADE WIPEOUT

By the end of the 1600s, French and English trading companies were shipping hundreds of thousands of beaver pelts across the Atlantic Ocean every year. And then the pace picked up even more. In the 1790s beaver-pelt sales peaked, with close to half a million sold in most years of that decade. When things started to slow down in the 1800s, it was mainly because so many beavers had been killed that there were almost none left.

In the early days of the fur trade, most of the pelts were supplied by Indigenous Peoples who hunted beavers the way they always had, often using clubs or spears to

kill them. Many of these Peoples, including the Cree, Algonquin, Dene and Tahltan, snagged beavers with nets made out of strips of moose hide or plant fibers twisted into cords. Wooden traps, set on land or in the water, were also common. Ojibwa hunters sometimes used keen-nosed dogs to detect beavers hiding in bank dens.

As the number of Europeans and their descendants in North America increased, they got more actively involved in obtaining beaver pelts, mostly using imported traps made of wrought iron or steel. Although these traps were heavy to carry and tended to break if they froze, they became the standard gear for both Indigenous and non-Indigenous trappers. Then in the early 1800s a 17-year-old blacksmith from New York State came up with an improved trap design that was a game changer. Sewell Newhouse's reliable, lightweight traps were soon being mass-produced and sold all across the continent. They were terrific for trappers and terrible for beavers.

As the fur trade rolled across North America, the ponds, lakes and rivers emptied of beavers. The trappers cleaned out *colony* after colony, and when they had killed off all the beavers in one place, they moved on to the next. Beavers vanished completely from some areas. In others they became so scarce it was as if they didn't exist. The places where they managed to hang on were mostly far from human settlements. Everywhere else, the trappers kept on trapping until beavers were nothing but a memory.

At the start of the 20th century, the number of beavers in all of North America was probably in the low hundred thousands. That's less than 1 percent of their estimated population before Europeans arrived.

DISRUPTED TRADITIONS

Indigenous Peoples in North America were important partners in the transatlantic fur trade. Many of them provided pelts and shared their expert knowledge of beavers and other animals. They also shared their knowledge of the land, as they showed the Europeans how to survive in this unfamiliar place and guided their journeys. The earliest participants were those who lived near the east coast, including the Haudenosaunee, Huron-Wendat, Algonquin and Innu. As the fur trade expanded, it drew in nearly every Indigenous community in its path. While it brought community members some short-term gains, it also inflicted much long-term pain.

Because beavers were so widespread and common across North America, most Indigenous Peoples knew these animals well, hunted them on a regular basis and were grateful for their gifts. For some communities, the most important of these gifts was food, provided by the

beavers' nutritious meat and fatty tails. For others it was the fur, which could be fashioned into warm clothing and blankets. Many also valued the bones and teeth. For example, in what is now the Northwest Territories, Tłı̨chǫ craftspeople turned the beaver's chisel-like incisors into special knives for making wooden snowshoe frames. On the west coast, the Coast Salish carved designs into those big front teeth and used them as dice for gambling games.

In addition to being used in these practical ways, beavers were, and still are, culturally significant to many Indigenous Peoples. The Tlingit, Tsimshian, Haida, Huron-Wendat, Haudenosaunee, Anishinaabe, Menominee, Mojave and others revere them as clan animals. The Niitsitapi (members of the Blackfoot Confederacy) refrained from killing beavers because the beaver, or ksik-stakii, holds a place of honor in their religion and culture and plays a leading role in the Niitsitapi story of the world's creation. In a number of Indigenous societies, such as Innu and Ojibwa, hunters showed their respect for beavers they had killed through careful handling of the animals' bones.

Beaver fur on the backs and cuffs of these moose-hide mittens adds warmth and sheds snow. They were made by a Chipewyan-Métis woman living in the Northwest Territories.
MITTENS, JANE DRAGON, CHIPEWYAN-MÉTIS CULTURE, 1990 CANADIAN MUSEUM OF HISTORY, VI-D-265 A-B, S94-33489

Traditional Coast Salish gambling games use beaver incisors as dice. A set of these dice usually consists of four teeth. Some have lines and dots carved into the white sides, and some are left plain.
DICE, 2003 OR EARLIER CANADIAN MUSEUM OF HISTORY, 2004.18.1100, IMG2010-0054-0073-DM

Depending on their specific customs, hunters returned the bones to the water, burned them or hung them in trees.

Unfortunately, the slaughter of beavers for the fur trade disrupted these traditions and left many Indigenous communities without an important source of meat, fur and other commodities. Indigenous Peoples were distressed by these changes and felt angry and sad about the way beavers were being treated, but their views were rarely listened to or valued by non-Indigenous power holders.

BOUNCING BACK

A hundred years ago, most Canadian and American kids living outside of northern communities had never seen a beaver and had little hope of seeing one in their lifetime. If they came across a beaver dam, it was probably falling apart and leaking because there were no beavers left to repair it. Back then many people thought beavers were headed for extinction. Thankfully, they were wrong. Instead the species has made a remarkable recovery. In fact, it's one of North America's greatest conservation success stories.

Like most such stories, this one was written by people who noticed there was a problem, believed it could be solved and worked hard to put solutions in place. Since the main cause of the beaver's extreme decline was uncontrolled trapping, beaver advocates began by pushing for trapping regulations. In time governments came onside and declared that anyone who wanted to trap beavers had to apply for a license and follow rules that limited the number of animals they could kill. They also established reserves and parks that were completely off-limits to trappers. As these changes took effect, beavers began to bounce back from the brink of extinction.

At a beaver festival in Martinez, California, a girl celebrates the return of this keystone species.
CHERYL REYNOLDS

Trappers traditionally used hoops made from flexible branches to stretch and dry beaver pelts. This photo of a Quebec trapper's wife and daughter was taken in 1948. By then trappers were required to follow rules designed to give beaver populations a chance to recover.

A CHANGE OF HEART

One of the people who fought hardest in the early 1900s to convince governments that beavers were worth more to us alive than dead was a former trapper, Archibald Belaney. He might never have become a beaver conservationist if not for his wife, a Mohawk woman named Gertrude Bernard but better known as Anahareo. Archie, as his friends called him, was born and raised in England and didn't see his first beaver until he moved to Canada as an adventurous 17-year-old in 1906. In northern Ontario, he made friends with an Ojibwa family who taught him how to hunt and trap and survive in the wilderness. At that point there were still enough beavers in northern Ontario that a skilled trapper like Archie could make a living from selling their pelts.

Beavers were the greatest love of Archibald Belaney's life and prompted him to become a conservationist.
LOVAT DICKSON COLLECTION/LIBRARY AND ARCHIVES CANADA/PA-147582

Normally Archie stopped trapping before kits were born in the spring. But in 1928 he was short on cash and kept going into early June. He was in his canoe, pulling up his traps after bagging a few final beavers, when he heard kits mewing inside the nearby lodge. Unsure what to do, he tried to ignore the sound. The next day Anahareo insisted they return to the lodge, where they found a couple of tiny beavers swimming about aimlessly and uttering plaintive cries. Since Archie had killed their parents and older siblings, Anahareo said it was their responsibility to save the kits. Archie agreed, so he and Anahareo fished the orphaned pair out of the water and paddled back to camp. Before long McGinnis and McGinty, as they called the kits, had won their hearts.

Although Archie had always admired and appreciated the beavers he observed in the wild, it had not stopped him from trapping them. But once he started caring for the kits, he found he couldn't continue killing their relatives. Urged on by Anahareo, he vowed to quit trapping beavers and devote himself to saving this species. Sadly, though, he wasn't able to protect the two beavers that had changed his life. McGinnis and McGinty disappeared when they were about a year old, most likely caught by another trapper.

Around the time Archie experienced this change of heart, he started calling himself Grey Owl and claiming to have Indigenous ancestry through his mother. He pretended to have been born in northern Mexico, not England, and created a fictitious history for himself that included an Apache childhood. Archie's family and old friends certainly knew his true history, and most Indigenous people who met him saw through his lies, but he managed

Grey Owl and Anahareo called their one-room cabin at Prince Albert National Park "Beaver Lodge"—and encouraged their pet beavers to build an actual lodge half inside the cabin.
LIBRARY AND ARCHIVES CANADA/C-043147

Beaver Lodge still stands at the edge of Ajawaan Lake, SK. Visitors can hike to the cabin and go inside. If you see a beaver swim by, it might be a descendant of the ones that Grey Owl and Anahareo brought there in 1931.
FRANCES BACKHOUSE

to fool the rest of the world. Nowadays that kind of deceit wouldn't be acceptable or, probably, even possible. At the time, however, some of those who knew the truth chose to stay quiet because of how he was helping the beavers, while others had no public voice.

As Grey Owl, Archie wrote magazine articles and books about beavers, gave presentations about beavers and starred in films about beavers—and in this guise he became world-famous as a beaver champion. The first film he appeared in was a nine-minute, black-and-white silent movie called *The Beaver People*, which you can watch on Canada's National Film Board website. It looks old-fashioned now, but it was groundbreaking at the time. Before the 1930s no one had ever professionally filmed beavers in the wild. *The Beaver People* stars the second pair of beavers that Archie and Anahareo adopted. As the movie shows, Jelly Roll and Rawhide knew their names and would come when called.

In 1931 Canada's national park service hired Grey Owl to share his passion for beavers with the public. He and Anahareo moved to Prince Albert National Park in Saskatchewan and settled into a one-room cabin beside a secluded lake. Jelly Roll, Rawhide and their four new kits came with them. The beavers' lodge stood half inside the cabin and half outside. The animals entered and exited the lodge like beavers normally do, through an underwater tunnel. They also figured out how to open the cabin door and would come and go as they pleased. Mostly they were welcomed, but some of their habits tried even Grey Owl's patience. For instance, they thought a blanket-covered bed was the perfect place to stand and squeeze the water out of their fur after swimming.

A few years after they moved to the park, Anahareo and Grey Owl split up. She and their young daughter left, and Grey Owl's conservation work became his whole life. By the time he died, in 1938, the beaver's fortunes had turned, thanks in part to his steadfast commitment to their cause. Every summer hundreds of people had boated or hiked to Grey Owl's cabin to meet the renowned beaver man and his equally famous beavers. Thousands more had read his writings, seen his films or heard him talk about beavers during one of his lecture tours through Canada, the United States and England. He had reached people of all ages and from many countries and inspired them to take up the beaver's cause. Their support, in turn, helped persuade governments to control trapping.

BEAVER TALES
BEAVERS AROUND THE WORLD

THE EURASIAN BEAVER came closer to disappearing than the North American beaver did and was missing from most of its range for much longer. After centuries without this keystone species, wildlife managers began reintroducing beavers to the European continent in the 1920s. They have now returned *Castor fiber* to more than 26 countries. The re-beavering of Great Britain began more recently. In 2009 three beaver families were moved from Norway to Scotland. Since then others have been released in England and Wales. In both Europe and Britain, the beaver population is growing steadily.

Meanwhile, in China's far northwest, Chu Wenwen, a wildlife photographer and filmmaker in her twenties is working to protect a subspecies of *Castor fiber* known as the Sino-Mongolian beaver. Sino-Mongolian beavers live only along the Ulungur River, and there may be as few as 500 left. Wenwen's biologist father studied these animals, and she grew up following and learning from him. She uses her camera to raise awareness of the Sino-Mongolian beaver's plight and has started a nonprofit conservation organization.

Returning beavers to their historical homelands makes sense. Transferring them to places where they don't belong doesn't, but it has happened. In 1946 the Argentine government imported 20 beavers from Manitoba and set them free on a large island at the tip of South America so islanders could trap them and sell their pelts. While the trapping plan never took off, the beavers did. With no natural predators and plenty of food, their numbers soared. Eventually some of them swam to other islands and the mainland.

There are now between 70,000 and 110,000 beavers living in Argentina and neighboring Chile, and they are wreaking havoc on the environment. In North America and Eurasia, woody plants and beavers have existed together for millions of years. Trees on these continents have developed adaptations to help them avoid or quickly recover from beaver attacks, but South American trees lack these defenses. They also can't tolerate the flooding caused by damming. As a result, beavers are destroying native forests in their new home. So far, attempts to get rid of the invaders have failed, but biologists haven't given up on trying to solve the problem.

Introduced beavers have inflicted long-lasting damage on this wetland in Tierra del Fuego, Argentina.
CHERIE WESTBROOK

A Eurasian beaver makes its way to the river in the French city of Grenoble. Beavers were nearly absent from France for centuries. Now they are returning.
LAURENT GESLIN/MINDEN PICTURES

A prospective passenger tries out one of the crates that Scotty Heter designed for delivering beavers to the Idaho wilderness in 1948.
IDAHO DEPARTMENT OF FISH AND GAME

HAPPY LANDINGS

New trapping regulations were just the start of the beaver's recovery. Once the pressure eased off, the survivors got busy rebuilding. In places that had plenty of beaver food but few beavers, litters were often large. When those kits grew up and left home, it was easy for them to find vacant territory and start adding their own offspring to the population.

Juvenile beavers in search of a place to settle can make epic journeys. They've been known to travel 30 miles (48 kilometers) or more on their way to a new address. But the loss of beavers in many parts of North America was so extensive that the blank spaces on the map were a long way from existing beaver colonies. It was going to take many generations of wandering juveniles to reach those remote areas. In the 1940s, some people who were concerned about the lack of beavers decided to speed up the process by catching beavers in areas where they were abundant and moving them to areas that had lost their populations. This conservation strategy is called *reintroduction*. Wildlife managers still use it today to help beavers in some regions.

In the mid-1940s the Idaho Department of Fish and Game started moving beavers into a rugged wilderness area. Beavers headed for a reintroduction site usually make the trip in the back of a truck, but there were no roads into this area, so the department used horses and mules to carry the beavers' crates. However, they soon discovered that these smelly, restless passengers made the pack animals nervous and hard to control. The long, hot, bumpy rides were also hard on the beavers.

Everyone agreed there had to be a better way to deliver the beavers. Elmo Heter, an Idaho conservation officer who went by the nickname Scotty, used his imagination and ingenuity to come up with one. After much study and experimentation, Scotty designed a suitcase-like wooden box that was attached to a parachute by ropes that held it shut while in the air. When the box touched down, the parachute collapsed, the ropes loosened, and the box opened. Each box was big enough to hold two adult beavers.

To test his invention with live cargo, Scotty enlisted the help of a large male beaver named Geronimo. He conducted the trials at an airfield. At first Geronimo scrambled out of the box the moment it opened on the ground. Scotty's assistants would then guide him back into his travel compartment and lug it over to the plane for another flight. After a while Geronimo got so used to the routine that he would crawl back into the box as soon as he saw the handlers coming.

Once the system was perfected, Geronimo's reward was a one-way trip to a mountain meadow where he

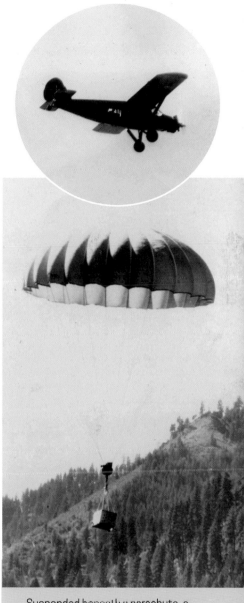

Suspended beneath a parachute, a box holding two beavers floats to the ground in Idaho. A conservation officer tossed the beaver boxes out of the airplane from an altitude of 500 to 800 feet (152 to 244 meters). IDAHO DEPARTMENT OF FISH AND GAME

Tulalip tribal member Kaiser Moses gives a thumbs-up as biologist Zoe Hayes weighs a beaver held in a live trap. The Tulalip Beaver Project in Washington State captures "nuisance" beavers and relocates them to places where they are more appreciated.
BENJAMIN DITTBRENNER, UNIVERSITY OF WASHINGTON

could go back to being a wild beaver with no bothersome humans around. Three female beavers made the trip with him. They immediately sauntered out and began exploring their landing site, but Geronimo didn't budge until he finally realized that this time he was free to go.

Altogether the Idaho Fish and Game Department air-dropped 76 beavers in the fall of 1948. One unlucky individual squirmed out of an improperly closed box in midair and jumped or fell to his death. The rest of the parachuting beavers survived the strange journey and seemed content with their new homes. When Scotty flew over the drop sites a year later, he saw that his recruits had built dams, lodges and food caches at all of them, and there have been beavers there ever since.

FROM RARE TO RARING TO GO

No one knows exactly how many beavers live in North America today. It's hard to count an animal whose population is so widespread and that lives in lots of out-of-the-way places. But it's clear that North America's current beaver numbers are still much lower than they were before Europeans arrived. Beavers are plentiful in some areas, but scarce or nonexistent in many others where they used to be common.

The parts of North America where they're struggling the most to make a comeback are also some of the driest, such as the western plains and deserts. It has always been more challenging for beavers to live in places with limited amounts of water. As our climate changes, the challenges are increasing, and so is the importance of having beavers in arid areas. You'll read more about that in chapter 4.

Beavers use their nimble front paws for many purposes, from manipulating building materials to grooming. This beaver is holding a morsel of food while dining in the water.
RUSTY COHN

Where there's an abundance of water (and food), the situation is quite different. Beaver populations have boomed in many such areas over the past century. Prince Albert National Park is a good example of how quickly beavers can increase when conditions are right. When Jelly Roll, Rawhide and their four kits moved there with Grey Owl and Anahareo in 1931, there were fewer than 500 other beavers in the park. Twenty years later there were at least 15,000. Once wolf populations caught up with this new food source, the park's beaver numbers dropped, but only slightly, and beavers continue to thrive there today.

JUSTIN BEAVER MOVES TO THE CITY

Biologists estimate that the number of beavers across the continent is now back into the tens of millions. No one expected beaver populations to grow so rapidly, and people were doubly surprised when beavers started to show up in cities. It turns out beavers don't mind making their homes next to busy streets surrounded by tall buildings. Human hustle and bustle is fine as long as the beavers have water to live in and plants, preferably woody ones, to eat and

This artificial wetland in a small park in Vancouver, BC, wasn't built by or for beavers, but they have happily settled there.
FRANCES BACKHOUSE

build with. Beavers have even made themselves at home in North America's largest metropolis, New York City.

When Europeans first came to North America, the area that is now New York City was prime beaver habitat. The fur traders quickly scooped up all the brown gold, and soon there were no more beavers. Later, New Yorkers paved over the city's creeks and dumped garbage and pollutants into its rivers, including the Bronx, which became unfit for beavers and most other living things.

In the 1990s concerned citizens began cleaning up the Bronx River. They hoped a healthier environment would allow some fish and wildlife to return. They weren't anticipating any beavers, but in 2006 one appeared and soon began building a lodge in a riverbank in the middle of the city. It was the first beaver seen in New York City in more than 200 years.

The biologists who first identified that pioneering beaver called it José. In 2010 it was joined by a companion. Fans nicknamed that one Justin Beaver. So far, José and Justin are the only members of their species who have settled in New York City, but they've proved that no city is too big for beavers.

A couple of beavers in a place that hasn't had any around for centuries gets people excited. When two becomes 200 or 2,000, excitement often turns to alarm. Sooner or later, people start complaining that there are too many beavers. If we could ask the beavers for their opinion, they might say the same thing about humans. They might also point out that they were here first and are just trying to reclaim their territory.

Must having beavers back always lead to conflict? Can't we all just get along? Read on to find out.

The beaver on this tile in the Astor Place Subway Station in New York City pays tribute to 19th-century fur trader John Jacob Astor and to the many beavers whose deaths made Astor a millionaire.
DEMERZEL21/GETTY IMAGES

BEAVER BACKERS

A GREAT-GRANDMOTHER'S WISH

Eric Collier stands by a restored beaver pond on the Chilcotin Plateau.
IMAGE FROM *THREE AGAINST THE WILDERNESS*
COPYRIGHT © 2007 BY THE ESTATE OF ERIC COLLIER.
REPRINTED WITH PERMISSION OF TOUCHWOOD EDITIONS.

ONE DAY WHEN VEASY COLLIER was 13, a pair of game wardens showed up out of the blue at his family's wilderness homestead. They had a couple of tin boxes in the back of their pickup truck. Brimming with excitement, Veasy watched the wardens carry the boxes to a pond near his family's log cabin and tip the contents into the water. Two beavers emerged—the first ones Veasy had ever seen.

As Veasy later recalled, the beavers' arrival was "a big deal." It meant that he and his parents had finally fulfilled his great-grandmother Lala's last wish, which was to have beavers returned to her family's lands.

Lala was a member of the Tsilhqot'in First Nation, whose territory encompasses an area of central British Columbia now called the Chilcotin Plateau. She was born around 1830, about the time the fur trade and European settlers reached this area. She witnessed big changes to her people's way of life during her early childhood. When she was 15, she gave up her Tsilhqot'in name, Chesahatna, and married a white rancher.

The Collier family's abandoned log cabin stands on a triangle of land where Meldrum Creek enters Madden Lake on its way to the Fraser River.
FRANCES BACKHOUSE

Veasy's mother, Lillian, was one of Lala's grandchildren. His father, Eric, was an Englishman who had immigrated to Canada at 17. Eric met and married Lillian a few years later.

Eric learned a lot about his new home from Lala, who was nearly 100 years old by then. They often talked about Meldrum Creek, which ran through the heart of Lala's family's traditional hunting grounds. When she was a child, beaver ponds along the creek had been home to enormous trout and abundant wildlife, including muskrats, minks and otters. In spring and fall, migrating ducks and geese had covered the water. But those days were over. Fur seekers had killed off the beavers, and the ponds had dried up. Lala wanted Eric and Lillian to go and live by Meldrum Creek and "give it back the beavers."

In 1931, when Veasy was two, he and his parents did move to Meldrum Creek, but there were no beavers around for hundreds of miles, and they had no idea where to find any. Eventually they decided to repair the broken beaver dams themselves. At least that would put water back into the ponds.

It took Eric, Lillian and seven-year-old Veasy weeks to fix up their first dam. Using only hand tools and muscle power, they felled trees, sawed them up and dragged the pieces into place. Veasy's main job was pushing a wheelbarrow filled with dirt that he helped pack in tight. When the next rains came, the old beaver pond began to refill. Then the first ducks splashed down. Success!

After that the Colliers rebuilt a dozen more dams, but they kept hoping to get some four-legged engineers to take over the work. The game wardens eventually heard about their project and managed to find some spare beavers for them. Two was all it took. Although Lala didn't live to see the beavers' return, she would have been happy to know that today their descendants are once again common on the Chilcotin Plateau.

The return of beavers to Meldrum Creek raised the water level in Madden Lake. And more water brought more cattails and water lilies to feed the beavers. These days there are several beaver lodges in Madden Lake.
FRANCES BACKHOUSE

Dozens of pointy white aspen stumps are scattered across this beaver worksite beside the Yukon River. The beavers who felled the trees live in a large bank den nearby.
FRANCES BACKHOUSE

4
LIVING WITH BEAVERS

THE TROUBLE WITH BEAVERS

How would you feel if someone hurt your dog? Or cut down your favorite tree? Or closed off the only road to your best friend's house? I'm guessing you'd be upset. Well, what if that someone was a beaver? Would that change how you felt?

Although beavers are special animals with unique talents, some people consider them pests. Of course, beavers don't mean to be a nuisance. They're simply doing what comes naturally, but there's no denying that they can make trouble for their human neighbors.

One of the most common complaints about beavers is that they fell trees we would prefer to see alive and upright. These might be cottonwoods growing along a river in a city park or fruit trees in an orchard. A single special tree, like the beloved willow someone's grandmother planted 50 years ago, or the best maple for climbing at the cottage. To beavers, they're all just a source of building material and food.

Beaver damming sometimes floods walking paths in Mary S. Young Park in West Linn, OR. A community organization called Beaver Ambassadors helps people understand why it's important to share such places with beavers.
FRANCES BACKHOUSE

People also object when flooding caused by beavers creates inconvenient or dangerous situations. Beavers love to build dams in *culverts*—pipes that allow water to run under roads or railway tracks. This is totally understandable. From a beaver's point of view, a roadbed with a culvert running through it is a ready-made dam that just needs a bit of work to block the hole. But plugged culverts often cause flooding and washouts. In other situations, enthusiastic damming can raise water levels so much that beaver ponds overflow into yards, gardens or farm fields. High water is great for beavers, but not so good for people who want to use the submerged land or flooded buildings.

TOO CLOSE FOR COMFORT

Because beavers have a strong instinct to defend themselves against any animal that looks like a wolf, they occasionally attack swimming dogs. The beaver's sharp incisors are formidable weapons that can inflict serious or even fatal injuries. Beavers attack only when they feel threatened. They are especially protective when their kits are out of the lodge. It's no use trying to tell a beaver that your dog is just cooling off or chasing the ball you threw for it.

To keep everyone safe, it's best to keep dogs out of the water if there are beavers around.

Another occasional complaint about beavers is that they're responsible for an illness known as beaver fever. The proper name for this ailment is giardiasis, but beaver fever is catchier and easier to say, so that's what it's often called, even though it's unfair to blame it on them. Giardiasis is caused by a microorganism called *Giardia*. These tiny parasites live in the guts of many kinds of animals, including beavers and humans. They're passed along when feces from an infected animal get into a water system and another animal comes in contact with that water. Millions of people around the world get sick with giardiasis every year, and most of them live nowhere near beavers. In North America, most *Giardia* victims pick up the parasite by drinking tap water that hasn't been properly purified or by splashing around in an infected swimming pool or water park.

For humans, a bout of giardiasis is a horrible experience. If you're lucky, you'll only have stomach cramps and diarrhea. Severe infections bring on chills, fever, headaches and vomiting. Thank goodness it's treatable. Although beavers don't seem to get sick from *Giardia*, they can be a link in the infection chain. To be on the safe side, you should never drink straight from a beaver pond or any other untreated water source.

Whatever our concerns, when we label beavers as troublemakers it usually means trouble for the beavers. Many people think the best way to solve their beaver problems is to get rid of the beavers. Unfortunately, when we get rid of beavers we lose out on beaver benefits, including habitat creation, community building and water stewardship.

A typical adult beaver weighs about the same as a Labrador retriever, like the one shown here.
SERGEY RYUMIN/GETTY IMAGES

RESERVOIRS, SPEED BUMPS AND WATER FILTERS

A steward is someone who manages and takes care of something. Beavers are outstanding water stewards, and in this time of climate crisis, that's more important than ever. If we give beavers room to live, they can be our climate-change allies, helping to ease the impact of both drier and wetter conditions.

One way beavers manage and take care of water is by storing it. Water held in beaver ponds is easy to see, but beaver engineering also increases underground water storage. When water collects in a pond instead of rushing downstream, it has time to seep into the ground around it and raise the *water table*. The pond is like a sink, and the

We can't see the water table, but we can see its effect on vegetation, especially in dry regions. The lush greenery bordering this creek shows how the creek raises the water table on both sides.
NICK WEBER, ANABRANCH SOLUTIONS

surrounding land is like a giant sponge that sucks up moisture and then slowly releases it. During periods of drought, this slow release keeps streams flowing and *groundwater* within reach of plant roots. As a result, plants don't go thirsty and the animals that eat them don't go hungry. Fish, frogs, ducks and other water-dependent creatures don't lose their homes. And our taps don't run dry.

Water stored by beavers also helps fight wildfires. Since water doesn't burn, the saturated soil around beaver ponds, and the ponds themselves, can put the brakes on raging fires. For animals fleeing flames, beaver-created wetlands are a refuge.

Too much water from heavy rainfall or rapid snowmelt can be as big a problem as too little water, and beavers can help in this regard as well. Dams and ponds slow water flow the way speed bumps slow vehicles on city streets, and this reduces downstream flooding. Although extreme downpours sometimes destroy beaver dams, beavers work hard to repair any damage as quickly as possible, and they usually succeed.

Another way beavers act as water stewards is by making streams clearer and cleaner. When water is slowed down by a dam, sediment particles settle out and sink to the bottom of the pond behind the dam. Sediment is basically pulverized bits of dirt, which scour like sandpaper as they're carried downstream. Decreasing the amount of sediment in streams reduces bank erosion and creates healthier conditions for fish. Beaver dams also help clean up pollution from fertilizers or pesticides that get flushed off farm fields and into waterways. Like sediments, these contaminants settle out in beaver ponds, where microbes and plants break them down.

After a forest fire, beaver wetlands often stand out as green oases in the blackened landscape.
JOE WHEATON, ANABRANCH SOLUTIONS

CASTOR FACT

Canada's first postage stamp, issued in 1851, portrayed a beaver crouched on a bank beside a stream. It was the first time any country's post office put an animal on a stamp.

HODAGMEDIA/GETTY IMAGES

A sign on the road into Ellis Bird Farm in Alberta warns drivers to go slow.
FRANCES BACKHOUSE

COEXISTENCE MEANS EVERYONE WINS

During the centuries when beavers were rare or absent across most of North America, humans took over a lot of their territory. We drained swamps, plowed up beaver meadows, straightened out creeks and cut down forests. Where beavers once lived, we established farms and ranches and built towns and cities. Along the way, we lost track of all the advantages we gained from having beavers around. We also got used to a beaverless world and came to think of this as the natural state of affairs. Now beavers are returning to their old hangouts and trying to get things back to their idea of normal. Sometimes that causes conflict.

The conventional response to beavers doing things we don't approve of is to remove the offenders. This solution may work in the short term but nearly always fails in the long term. That's because good beaver habitat won't stay empty forever. Kick out the current residents, and it's only a matter of time before new home seekers come along and spot the vacancy sign. This approach is never good for beavers either. Too often they are simply killed. A kinder option is to live-trap and relocate them to a new home, but suitable relocation sites can be hard to find. There isn't as much beaver habitat around as there once was, and in some parts of North America, beavers have already filled up what's left. If a trapped beaver is dropped off in territory belonging to other beavers, they won't let it stay.

Fortunately, there are more effective and humane solutions, and they're catching on. These alternatives involve leaving beavers where they are but preventing them from bothering their human neighbors. The beavers get a comfortable home, and we get beaver benefits. Living together, or coexisting, means everyone wins.

Ethan Arnold plants a willow to improve habitat for beavers in Martinez, CA.
SUZI ESZTERHAS/MINDEN PICTURES

BEAVER TALES
WORTH A DAM

When graffiti artist Tim Hon moved to Martinez, he was amazed to discover beavers living in the middle of the town. He painted this mural to share his excitement about the beavers with others.
AARON JOB/MARTINEZ NEWS-GAZETTE

In 2007 beavers took up residence on a creek that runs right through downtown Martinez, in Northern California. They were the first beavers seen in the city in at least a century. Some people were thrilled. Others feared that beaver dams on Alhambra Creek would cause dangerous and costly flooding.

From the moment Heidi Perryman caught her first glimpse of the newcomers, she was a fan. She had only ever seen one beaver before. Now she could head downtown every day and get to know a whole beaver family. On many evenings she joined crowds on a bridge that spans the creek and shared their delight in watching the adorable kits.

Meanwhile, the city council kept worrying about flooding, and it finally voted to exterminate the dam builders. Heidi and other citizens of all ages leaped to the beavers' defense. They circulated petitions, wrote letters, held rallies, did media interviews and spoke out at public meetings. Together they convinced the city to install a flow device to control the water level behind the dam. That bought the beavers some time, but their fate remained undecided.

Determined to save the beavers, Heidi formed an advocacy group called Worth A Dam and organized a beaver festival in a park next to Alhambra Creek. "It occurred to me," she says, "that it would be a lot harder

Beaver fans often gather on this footbridge over Alhambra Creek to watch the action below. On this occasion, Heidi Perryman had it to herself.
SARAH KOENIGSBERG, COURTESY OF *THE BEAVER BELIEVERS*

Heidi Perryman, proudly wearing her Worth A Dam T-shirt.
SARAH KOENIGSBERG, COURTESY OF *THE BEAVER BELIEVERS*

to kill the beavers after we threw a party for them." She was right. The beavers were allowed to stay.

Not only has Alhambra Creek never flooded since the beavers moved back, but they've also transformed it. Instead of dwindling to a lifeless trickle each summer, it flows year round and supports a dynamic ecosystem. Returned species include steelhead trout, river otters and minks. When you throw a party for beavers, their friends are sure to show up.

Since 2007 more than two dozen kits have been born and raised on Alhambra Creek. The Martinez Beaver Festival is now an annual event, and Worth A Dam continues to run school programs, wire-wrap trees and plant willows along the creek to replenish the beavers' food supply. Heidi also helps people all over North America who are trying to protect beavers in their own towns and cities.

TRICK OR TREAT

When a beaver dam causes flooding problems, tearing down the dam is pointless. The beavers will build a new one in short order. If we want to coexist, a better solution is to lower the water below flooding level while ensuring that the pond remains deep enough to meet the beavers' needs. This can be done by installing a flow device.

A flow device is a long pipe that runs through or over the top of a dam and creates a permanent leak. The upstream end of the pipe is set far out in the pond and fenced off with wire so the beavers can't get close enough to hear or feel water flowing into the pipe or plug it. They may detect water coming out of the pipe on the downstream side of the dam, but they won't know where it's coming from or be able to stop it. Flow devices are often referred to as pond levelers because they regulate water levels.

Installing flow devices is wet work! After placing the intake end of the pipe into the cage, the installer will submerge it to the desired water level. The other end of the pipe will go through the dam, which isn't visible in this photo.
TIMOTHY SEXAUER

This culvert protector will prevent beavers from blocking the culvert opening and flooding the road above it. JULIE NELSON

Clogged road culverts call for a different approach. The key to coexistence in these situations is to keep the beavers away from the culvert so they can't dam it up. A well-designed exclusion fence, paired with a pipe system, will achieve that goal.

Skip Lisle is one of the people who led the way in developing these kinds of beaver-management tools. Skip's passion for peaceful coexistence began when he was growing up in rural Vermont in the 1960s and '70s. He and his parents often went for evening drives to watch beavers in nearby wetlands. Later, beavers moved into a pond on his family's property, and he got a fascinating firsthand view of how they turned it into a thriving ecosystem.

Skip Lisle stands on top of the pipe that will siphon water out of a beaver pond. His goal is to keep the water level high enough that beavers can live comfortably there and low enough to prevent conflicts with people.
DOUG KNUTSON, WINDSWEPT PRODUCTIONS

When Skip was 13, beavers dammed a road culvert on his family's land. To prevent them from flooding the road and earning themselves a death sentence, he cleared out the sticks and caged off the culvert opening with some old garden fencing. That successful experiment was the beginning of a long career dedicated to helping people solve their beaver problems without harming any beavers. Over the years he has designed, built and installed more than a thousand culvert protectors and flow devices and inspired many other people to follow in his footsteps.

Skip's trademarked name for the fence-and-pipe system he invented to keep culverts clear of dams is the Beaver Deceiver. Deceiving beavers might seem unfair, but it's better than the alternative. Tricking them into changing their behavior keeps humans happy and beavers alive.

HELPING BEAVERS HELP US

BEAVER BACKERS

MEET AVA, KAJA AND ILA, a teenage trio of Methow Beaver Project (MBP) volunteers. The MBP is based in the Methow Valley in northeastern Washington State. This dry region has a beaver shortage, yet people don't always appreciate the beavers that are around. When conflicts arise, the MBP offers coexistence solutions, or if necessary, moves the unwanted animals to where they won't annoy anyone. Since the project began in 2008, the MBP has relocated more than 400 beavers.

Methow Beaver Project volunteers carry a beaver through a recently burned forest to the site where it will be released. JULIE NELSON

HELPING BEAVERS HELP US

AVA MOTT got involved after visiting the MBP booth at a school careers day when she was 13. "I was super interested in working with animals at that time," she says. "Once I started, I learned a lot about why beavers are super beneficial to the environment around our community and how they help create wetlands and habitat for other animals, and that's why I continued." When I spoke with her, she was into her fifth summer of volunteering.

The MBP generally releases beavers in male-female pairs. Beavers waiting for a mate or a suitable release site stay at a fish hatchery that has spare room. Long concrete tanks, called raceways, substitute for ponds. Huts made of concrete blocks serve as lodges.

Ava's main volunteer job is feeding the beavers at the hatchery. Wearing hip waders, she jumps down into the raceways and quietly visits each occupied lodge. She rinses food bowls and doles out food pellets, plus, when they're available, freshly cut aspen branches. She also records how much her charges eat and spends a few minutes observing them so she can report any health concerns to the project biologists.

"I love being able to watch the beavers interact and learn more about each of their personalities," she says. Some are shy, others are friendly. She particularly remembers one of the first beavers she worked with who soaked her with a big tail slap. "He was very spunky!"

AVA MOTT

HELPING BEAVERS HELP US

BEAVER BACKERS

When **KAJA AAGAARD** came on board as a beaver feeder at 16, she was surprised by the size of the beavers. "They're a lot bigger than I imagined," she says. "When you actually see them in person, they're pretty huge."

The next summer Kaja spent a week working with a graduate student who was studying beaver habitat in the Methow Valley. They put in long days, hiking around the backcountry and collecting data. Most areas they visited had signs of past beaver occupancy but no beavers. When they finally found a site where beavers were living, it was distinctly different. "The water was a lot more slow-moving," Kaja recalls. "There were a lot of salmon too. That's what stood out to me. At the other sites there were no fish around."

Doing fieldwork for the first time "was cool," she says. She's now studying biology at college but still helps out at the hatchery when she's back in the valley for the summer.

FRANCES BACKHOUSE

BEAVER BACKERS

HELPING BEAVERS HELP US

ILA NEWMAN started helping with the MBP when she was 12, and it quickly became a major part of her seventh-grade homeschooling. That year she set up motion-activated cameras to monitor winter beaver activity and conducted a beaver pond water-quality study. When I met her in August, she was already planning her eighth-grade beaver projects.

One of Ila's first MBP activities was assisting with a beaver release. The crew drove "way, way up a dirt road" with the caged beaver in the back of their truck. After parking, they took turns working in pairs to lug the heavy load down a steep slope, hefting it over fallen trees and pushing through brush. When they reached their destination, they set the cage in the stream and opened the door. "He kind of waddled out and got in the water and immediately slapped his tail at us," Ila says, "and then he swam off."

Ila also helped construct a *beaver dam analog (BDA)* to set the stage for a future beaver release. As part of a team of volunteers, she spent a morning weaving willow branches between posts that had been erected across a creek. As they wove, the dam started working, and before long the water had risen to the top of her boots.

"What I like most about working with beavers," Ila says, "is that they are so helpful to our environment, and they likely have no idea!"

FRANCES BACKHOUSE

TREE-SHARING TACTICS

When it comes to protecting trees from beavers, there are several coexistence solutions available. The most common is to wrap a cylinder of heavy wire fencing (not flimsy chicken wire!) around the base of the trunk. The cylinder should be at least 4 feet (1.2 meters) tall and should leave some room for the tree to grow. In places with snowy winters, the top of the fence should be 2 feet (0.6 meters) above the highest snow level.

Another tactic is to stir sand into house paint and apply the mixture to the trunks of treasured trees. Beavers don't like gnawing on grit and will leave the painted trees alone. Like wire mesh, the sand-paint must extend higher than beavers can reach. The recommended formula is 20 ounces of sand per gallon of paint (approximately 140 grams of sand per liter). If you pick a color that matches the tree bark, the paint is barely noticeable.

Sherry and Ted Guzzi sand-paint an aspen tree. They carefully picked a paint color that blends in with the color of the bark. TOOGEE SIELSCH, SIERRA WILDLIFE COALITION

A beaver dam analog looks like a cross between a fence and a logjam.
NICK WEBER, ANABRANCH SOLUTIONS

Obviously if we want beavers to stick around, we can't completely lock the doors to their grocery and building-supply stores. Some of their preferred trees should be left unwired and unpainted.

We can also give beavers alternative sources of food and building materials to make up for the trees that have been declared off-limits. The most effective way to do this is to plant willows and other beaver-approved shrubby plants that grow rapidly and keep sprouting back no matter how many times the beavers cut them down. Sometimes there are also opportunities to serve up precut provisions, such as pruned branches, to supplement what the beavers gather for themselves.

KICK-STARTER DAMS

Reintroduction was an important part of beaver conservation during the first half of the 20th century. Later, as beaver populations grew and places to put them became harder to find, reintroduction efforts declined. Yet some parts of North America still have plenty of vacant beaver habitat. In recent years people who understand the value of putting beavers back where they belong have been leading a reintroduction revival. Sometimes the beavers reject the new site and go looking for a place more to their liking. Other times they settle right in. Biologists are studying both outcomes to try to increase the success rate.

One thing they've learned is that some vacant habitat needs to be renovated before beavers can move back. Streams that haven't had beavers in residence for a very long time can become badly damaged by erosion. If a stream channel is too deeply eroded, it's impossible for beavers to live there because they can't build dams that are

A boy looks over a beaver pond that was started with beaver dam analogs. The posts sticking out of the water in the background are part of a BDA he helped build.
JOE WHEATON, ANABRANCH SOLUTIONS

This new beaver dam analog has already raised the water on the upstream side to the knees of the construction crew members.
NICK WEBER, ANABRANCH SOLUTIONS

tall enough and strong enough to not get washed away. In these situations we can give beavers a boost by building starter dams, also known as beaver dam analogs.

The first, and hardest, step in building a BDA is pounding a line of wooden posts into place across the stream channel. The construction crew then weaves long sticks through this framework to create a barrier. Willow branches are ideal if they're available, but any kind of flexible branch will work. Finally, the builders shove handfuls of vegetation into any gaps and smear mud over the whole structure.

Like a real beaver dam, a BDA slows down the stream flow and causes sediment particles to settle out of the water. As the sediment piles up on the bottom, the streambed rises, and the stream becomes shallower and more beaver-friendly. At this point the beavers can take over and carry on the task of restoration.

Additional dam construction by the beavers keeps raising the streambed, which in turn raises the water table on either side of the stream. That water then starts quenching the thirst of nearby plants. As the greenery along the stream grows back, insects, amphibians, reptiles, birds and mammals return. The beavers' work changes the shape of the stream as well, making it wider and more meandering and creating side channels and pools. That's good news for fish.

BDAs can also help beavers recolonize streams that aren't eroded. In these situations, their purpose is to create ready-made ponds so newly arrived beavers can stay out of reach of predators while they're settling in.

Eventually all BDAs either get integrated into real beaver dams or fall apart. They aren't intended to last forever, just to get the expert dam builders back on the job.

Emily Wilde helped build BDAs on her family's ranch in Idaho. She later caught this cutthroat trout in one of the newly created beaver ponds. Working on this project inspired her to pursue a university degree in environmental studies.
CASEY WILDE

WATCHING BEAVERS IN THE WILD

Ever since I was a kid, I've loved getting to know wild animals by looking for tracks and other signs and watching them go about their lives. However, I didn't see my first beaver in the wild until I was in my late teens. Beavers were still uncommon when I was young, and I also didn't know where, when or how to observe them. Now I do, and I enjoy every opportunity I get.

If you're lucky, you might see a beaver on land, usually working or grooming itself, but sightings of beavers in the water are more common. You can watch them from the shore or from a canoe, kayak or rowboat. The key to success is to be quiet and patient. Even urban beavers who are used to putting up with noisy, lively humans prefer not to be disturbed. Remember too that dogs and beavers don't mix, especially when there are young kits around. If you have a dog with you, keep it under control and out of the water.

Because we humans have poor night vision, our prime beaver-watching times are at dusk and dawn. The best

The beaver's webbed back feet make distinctive tracks.
PAUL STAROSTA/GETTY IMAGES

season for daytime watching is fall, when beavers are extra busy preparing for winter and are more likely to be working during the day.

A swimming beaver is like an iceberg—most of its mass is hidden underwater. From a distance, you may spot its wake before you make out the visible parts of its head, back and tail. When the beaver gets closer, you'll probably see it raising its nose and sniffing the air. While you're using your eyes to study the beaver, it's using its powerful sense of smell to try to figure out who and what you are. An explosive tail slap will tell you that the beaver has decided you are a threat or, at least, too strange a creature to trust. But wait a bit, and the beaver may resurface to investigate further.

SIGNS AND TRACKS

Even when beavers remain out of sight, you can find plenty of evidence of their activities. When you come across a dam, lodge or bank den, see if you can tell whether it's currently in use. Fresh mud is a sure sign of recent maintenance work. In fall and winter, a food cache near a lodge is another clue that beavers are living there.

Pointy tree stumps and piles of wood chips are obvious indicators that beavers are around or have been in the past. But it takes sharp eyes to pick out the beaver's angled cuts on the stems of willows or other shrubs.

As you walk along the shore, watch for drag trails (paths made by the beavers hauling branches to the water), scent mounds (castoreum-scented mud pies) and tracks. Perfect footprints are hard to find because the beaver's trailing tail usually blurs them. However, its large webbed hind feet make even partially erased tracks easy to identify.

If you want a souvenir of your visit to a beaver neighborhood, chances are you'll be able to find a chew stick—a smooth length of wood with the bark peeled off and telltale tooth marks on one or both ends. A fresh chew stick will be gleaming white. The one that sits on my windowsill is bronzed with age and brings back warm memories whenever I look at it.

A DAY TO CELEBRATE BEAVERS

Did you know that April 7 is International Beaver Day? Beavers: Wetlands & Wildlife (BWW), an organization based in New York State, started the tradition of honoring beavers on that date in 2009. BWW chose April 7 because it was the birthday of Dorothy Richards, the woman whose work led to the organization's creation. Dorothy was born in 1894, when beavers had almost disappeared from North America. At 41 she read *Pilgrims of the Wild*, one of Grey Owl's books about beavers, which moved her to turn her property in the Adirondack Mountains into a beaver refuge. She called it Beaversprite Sanctuary.

A beaver's favorite feeding spot is often marked by a scattering of peeled and discarded sticks.
CHUCK GARRETT

A brightly colored drawing chalked on a sidewalk expresses the artist's appreciation for beavers.
CHERYL REYNOLDS

Dorothy devoted the rest of her life to studying the beavers who shared her home and educating people about the importance of beavers. During the 50 years she ran the sanctuary, she welcomed more than 100,000 visitors.

There are many ways you can celebrate beavers on International Beaver Day (or any other day). To get you started, here are five things to do on your own or with friends or family.

1. Hike around a beaver pond or along a stretch of river where beavers live. Look for beaver signs along the way and spend some quiet moments near the lodge or dam, watching for beavers swimming or working.
2. Visit the beavers at your local zoo or eco-park. Some, like the Oregon Zoo (in Portland) and the Montreal Biodôme, have windows in the enclosures that let you watch the beavers swimming underwater.
3. Work with the librarian at your school or public library to arrange a display of books about beavers.
4. Use your artistic talents to express your thoughts and feelings about beavers. Write a poem or a song, put on a play or puppet show, or create some beaver artwork.
5. Throw a party and serve beaver-themed food, such as beaver cupcakes or cookies, chocolate lodges or a carved watermelon beaver. It's easy to find recipes for all these treats online.

ANNA PYE

Kids decorating paper beavertails at a community event on Earth Day.
SHERRY GUZZI, SIERRA WILDLIFE COALITION

The annual Martinez Beaver Festival includes creek tours, information booths, street art and a parade.
CHERYL REYNOLDS

BEAVER BACKERS

MADELEINE MILLIGAN was born and raised in Fernie, a small town in southeastern British Columbia. She's always known beavers lived there too, but she was 15 before she really understood their importance. That's when the Elk River Alliance, a local conservation organization, came and talked to her 10th-grade science class about this keystone species.

"It was eye-opening, to say the least," Madeleine recalls. "I didn't appreciate just how much beavers contribute to the healthy functioning of the wider ecosystem."

Several creeks flow through Fernie, widening into wetlands in places and emptying into the Elk River. It's such good beaver habitat that there's even a Beaver Street in town. But until recently most residents regarded the rodents as nothing but trouble. The Elk River Alliance is trying to change that view and encourage coexistence by installing flow devices, fencing culverts and wire-wrapping trees to keep beavers from cutting them down.

Soon after the Alliance's school visit, Madeleine and her classmates spent a day protecting trees along the West Fernie Dike Trail, a popular riverside walking path. Working in teams, the 23 students secured cylinders of wire mesh around 35 large cottonwoods. Fifth and sixth graders from another Fernie school wrapped 20 more cottonwoods along the dike.

Across the river, in an area known as the Annex, the Alliance put up signs about the value of beavers and wetlands. A class of eighth and ninth graders at a third Fernie school wrote the text for one of them. It lists some of the animals that use the beaver-engineered Annex wetlands, from mayflies to moose, and describes how the wetlands filter stormwater so pollutants don't enter the river.

Madeleine lives near the West Fernie Dike and often walks her dog there. Occasionally she pauses to reattach a bit of loose wiring. The beavers have left the wrapped cottonwoods alone and seem satisfied with the smaller trees that were left unwrapped for them—proof that the students' handiwork is helping keep the peace between humans and beavers.

Madeleine Milligan is all smiles as she and Dylan Morgan put the finishing touches on a wire-wrapped cottonwood while classmate Emma Soetaert looks on.
BETH MILLIONS

Two Methow Beaver Project volunteers cart a beaver to its new home. Others follow, carrying aspen branches to leave at the release site. This gift of food and building materials will help the beaver settle in.
JULIE NELSON

HOW CAN YOU GIVE BEAVERS A BOOST?

If you'd like to help beavers throughout the year, begin by finding out what's happening with them in your area. Are they common or rare? How do people in your city, town or rural area regard beavers? If there are conflicts, how are they being resolved? Are there any good beaver-watching sites around? Are any local organizations working on beaver-conservation projects? Is there a wildlife facility nearby that rescues and rehabilitates orphaned and injured beavers? Once you've answered some or all of these questions, you'll have a better sense of what needs to be done and how you can chip in.

Beaver-boosting activities you could get involved in include:

1. **Hands-on work**, such as building BDAs or protecting trees with wire or sand-paint. These kinds of projects should always be led by people who have appropriate training and experience. If not done properly, they won't be effective and could even harm beavers or the environment. Check with conservation organizations or your local parks department to find out whether they're planning any beaver projects that need work-crew volunteers.

Wet weather doesn't bother
beavers—or keen beaver watchers.
ELYSSA KERR, BEAVERS NORTHWEST

2. **Citizen science research.** Look for an opportunity to participate in an organized research project. If you can't find one, contact a local conservation organization and see if someone there can connect you with a researcher who needs a helper. Or create your own project. If you're not sure how to do that, ask your teacher for advice.

3. **Educating the public** about beavers, the benefits they provide and how we can coexist with them. There are endless ways to do this. You could volunteer to staff a conservation organization's information table at community events or set up your own table. You could make a video and share it through social media. You could write a community newsletter article. You could get permission to paint a mural on a wall or building.

4. **Caring for beavers**. Many wildlife rescue centers welcome volunteers. They usually allow only qualified adults to handle injured or orphaned beavers, but they may appreciate assistance with other essential tasks, such as cleaning cages.

5. **Fundraising**. Conservation organizations and wildlife rescue centers are always grateful for donations. Pick one whose beaver work you would like to support and hold a fundraising event, perhaps on International Beaver Day.

Give it some thought and you may come up with more ideas. Whenever and however you take action, these radical rodents are always worth celebrating and helping. Because if we're there for beavers, they'll be there for us and all the other living things that benefit from their remarkable ecosystem engineering.

Wildlife rescue centers provide expert care and rehabilitation for animals like this orphaned beaver kit. Whenever possible, rescued animals are returned to the wild once they are able to survive on their own.
MELANIE WHALEN, CALGARY WILDLIFE REHABILITATION SOCIETY

With little more than mud and sticks, beavers shape the world in incredible ways.
STAN TEKIELA AUTHOR / NATURALIST / WILDLIFE PHOTOGRAPHER/GETTY IMAGES

GLOSSARY

Arctic tundra—the area north of the Arctic Circle where it's too cold and dry for trees to grow

bank den—a beaver burrow dug into the bank of a river or lake

beaver dam analog (BDA)—a human-built structure that spans a stream channel and mimics or reinforces a natural beaver dam

beaver meadow—a wet, grassy area on the site of a former beaver pond that has either filled with sediment or drained due to lack of dam maintenance

cambium—the soft, nutritious layer of bark found between the hard inner wood and tough outer bark of a tree or shrub

canal—a waterway constructed by beavers or humans

castoreum—a yellowish-brown substance used by beavers for scent-marking that is produced and stored in the castor sacs, which are tucked inside the beaver's body at the base of the tail

castorids—members of the beaver family (Castoridae)—"castorid" is the formal, scientific way of saying "beaver"

cellulose—the main material in the cell walls of plants. It is used to make paper, cellophane and other products.

citizen science—scientific research done by nonscientists, often working as partners with professional scientists

clinometer—a measuring tool used to determine slopes, heights and angles of landscape features, trees or other large objects while standing in one place

colony—members of a beaver family who share the same territory. Usually a colony consists of one pair of adults living with their kits and juvenile offspring.

culvert—a pipe that runs under a road or railway track and is open at both ends so water can flow through it

DNA—coded molecules found in every cell of every living thing to provide instructions for development, growth and reproduction. *DNA* stands for deoxyribonucleic acid.

ecosystem—a community of living things, along with the nonliving parts of their environment (such as water, soil and rocks), all linked together through nutrient cycles and energy flows

ecosystem engineer—a keystone species that influences its ecosystem by significantly changing its environment

food cache—food hidden in a secure storage place. A beaver food cache is a pile of leafy branches collected by beavers and anchored to the bottom of their pond near their lodge to provide food during winter.

groundwater—water in underground spaces within the soil and in the cracks in rocks. It comes from rain and melted snow soaking into the earth.

habitat—the place where a plant or animal makes its home and can get all the things it needs to survive, such as food, water and shelter

incisors—teeth located at the front of the mouth and designed for cutting and gnawing

keystone species—an animal or plant that has a very large influence on the health and functioning of its ecosystem. There are several kinds of keystone species, including ecosystem engineers and keystone predators.

lodge—the homes of beavers. A freestanding lodge is completely surrounded by water, and a bank lodge is built into the bank of a river or lake and is only partly bordered by water.

nocturnal—active at night

nutrients—substances that animals and plants require to live and grow

plankton—microscopic plants and animals that live in fresh or salt water

reintroduction—a conservation activity that returns members of an animal or plant species to places where that species used to live

semi-aquatic—living partly on land and partly in water

species—a group of closely related organisms that have similar characteristics and can breed to produce offspring

subspecies—a subgroup within a species. Different subspecies within a species usually live apart from each other.

trace fossil—the preserved evidence of something an ancient organism left behind, such as a footprint, burrow or imprint. It differs from a regular fossil, which is the preserved evidence of the organism itself.

tubers—thick, underground stems that send up new shoots. Only certain plants, such as water lilies and potatoes, have tubers.

water table—the underground area where all the cracks in rocks and spaces between soil particles are filled with water

JENNIFER VANDERHOOF

RESOURCES

Print

Collier, Eric. *Three Against the Wilderness*. Victoria, BC: TouchWood Editions, 2007.

Ryden, Hope. *Lily Pond: Four Years with a Family of Beavers*. New York, NY: William Morrow & Co, 1989.

Tournay, Audrey. *Beaver Tales: Audrey Tournay and the Aspen Valley Beavers*. Erin, ON: Boston Mills Press, 2003.

Video

Beaver: Back to the Future. A short documentary about how reintroducing beavers helps dry regions cope with climate change. vimeo.com/140201129

The Beaver People. A silent movie featuring Grey Owl and Anahareo and their beavers. nfb.ca/film/beaver_people

The Unknown Heroes of the Methow Valley. A short documentary about the Methow Beaver Project, made by Methow Valley high school student Koharu Yonebayashi. kunoichiproduction.com/films

Film

Beavers. A 1988 documentary originally filmed for IMAX.

Leave It to Beavers. A 2014 PBS documentary.

The Beaver Believers. An award-winning 2018 documentary.

The Beaver Whisperers. A 2013 CBC *The Nature of Things* documentary.

Online

Association for the Protection of Fur-Bearing Animals (The Fur-Bearers): thefurbearers.com/campaigns/living-wildlife/solutions/beavers

Beaver Deceivers: beaverdeceivers.com

Beaver Institute: beaverinstitute.org

Beaver Solutions: beaversolutions.com

Beavers Northwest: beaversnw.org

Koharu Yonebayashi films beavers for a documentary she made during her senior year of high school.
JULIE NELSON

Beavers: Wetlands & Wildlife: beaversww.org

Clark Fork Coalition (includes link to a GIS [geographic information system] story map about youth-crew beaver-habitat surveys):
clarkfork.org/young-citizen-scientists-make-their-mark

Hinterland Who's Who—Beaver: hww.ca/en/wildlife/mammals/beaver.html

Methow Beaver Project: methowbeaverproject.org

Occidental Arts & Ecology Center: oaec.org/projects/bring-back-the-beaver-campaign

Putting Beavers to Work for Watershed Resiliency and Restoration: rockies.ca/beavers

RSBP (information on beaver reintroduction in Great Britain): rspb.org.uk/our-work/our-positions-and-casework/our-positions/species/beaver-reintroduction-in-the-uk

Sierra Wildlife Coalition: sierrawildlife.org

The Beaver Coalition: beavercoalition.org

The Lands Council: landscouncil.org/beaver

West Linn Beaver Ambassadors: beaverambassadors.com

Worth A Dam: martinezbeavers.org/wordpress

For a complete list of references, visit the page for this book at orcabook.com.

Links to external resources are for personal and/or educational use only and are provided in good faith without any express or implied warranty. There is no guarantee given as to the accuracy or currency of any individual item. The author and publisher provide links as a service to readers. This does not imply any endorsement by the author or publisher of any of the content accessed through these links.

ACKNOWLEDGMENTS

This book is built on the foundations of many years of writing about beavers, including my first book on this subject (*Once They Were Hats: In Search of the Mighty Beaver*), a CBC *Ideas* radio documentary and several magazine articles. Along the way, so many people have helped me learn about beavers that I can't individually acknowledge all of them here. To everyone who contributed to laying the foundations, a collective and sincere thanks.

Equally heartfelt thanks to everyone whose beaver expertise I drew on this time around, especially Natalia Rybczynski, Cherie Westbrook and Glynnis Hood. Glynnis has been answering my beaver questions ever since I began swimming in this pond and gets an extra-big tail slap of appreciation for her generosity, knowledge, patience, good humor and encouragement.

My favorite part of writing this book was talking with the young people whose stories appear in it. Special thanks to Garrett Goulstone, Ila Newman, Ava Mott, Kaja Aagaard and Madeleine Milligan for sharing their beaver experiences with me. Thanks also to Julie Nelson, Sarah Bates, Nick Ehlers, Lily Haines, Emma Gregson, Catherine Off, Allison Ciancibelli, Christine Mullie and Sylvia Ayers for facilitating those conversations.

To Mike Callahan, Rusty Cohn, Ben Dittbrenner, Robin Ellison, Chuck Garrett, Ben Goldfarb, Sherry Guzzi, Lisa Hodge, Holly Kinas, Doug Knutson, Skip Lisle, Scott McGill, Steven Murschel, Heidi Perryman, Frank Rosell, Cheryl Reynolds, Judy and Jim Taylor-Atkinson, Jean Thie, Jennifer Vanderhoof, Melanie Whalen, Joe Wheaton, Maggie Winston, Steve Zack and the countless other

A beaver kit perches on a stick extending from the wall of its family home.
ROBERTCICCHETTI/GETTY IMAGES

beaver enthusiasts I connected with online or in person while working on this book, thank you for providing me with inspiration, insights and encouragement.

Big thanks to the photographers whose images enliven these pages, as well as everyone who shared photos that do not appear in the book. It was hard to choose from so many great contenders.

Thank you to Kirstie Hudson for inviting me to write this book and for her astute editing, to Dahlia Yuen for her fabulous design work, and to the entire Orca Book Publishers team for bringing it into being. Thanks also to my great-nephew Wren Audy for graciously agreeing to read my first draft and providing thoughtful feedback.

Once again, my literary agent made the business of book writing a bit easier; thank you, Carolyn Swayze, for all the years you've cheered me on.

As always, I am deeply grateful to Mark Zuehlke for supporting me on the home front and enthusiastically accompanying me on research trips whenever possible.

And finally, thank you to beavers everywhere for the critically important work they do and for giving us the pleasure of their company.

INDEX

*Page numbers in **bold** indicate an image caption.*

Aagaard, Kaja, 95, 97
adaptations: feet, 16, **18**, **31**, **106**; front paws, 28, 40, **41**, **77**; incisors, 8, 11, 65, 84, 115; senses, 20, 44, 106; for swimming, 14–16, **18**, 45; tail, **18**, **19**–20, **31**, 32
Anahareo, 68–71, 78
appearance, 2, 8–**9**, **15**, **85**
Argentina, beavers in, 72
artwork, **90**, **107**, 108; sculpture, **58**, 59
aspen, 7, 22, 27, 36, **82**, 99

bank dens, 13, 24, 114
beaver dam analog (BDA), 98, **100**, 101–103, 114
beaver dams: construction, 39–**40**, 44, **45**; in culverts, 84; dimensions, 42-43; and ecosystems, 81, 87, 103; purpose, 10, 11, 30, 39; and sediment 51-52, 87; and water management, 86-87; wildlife bridges, 56
beaver fever (giardiasis), 85
Beaverlodge (AB), **58**, 59
beaver meadows, **51**–52, 114
Beaver People, The (film), 70
beaver place-names, 59–61
Beavers: Wetlands & Wildlife (BWW), 107
beaver species: extinct, 8-9; living, 5-6
beaver trapping, 63–64, 66, **67**, 68-69

beaver watching, 1–2, **56**, 105–107
behaviors: care of young, 13, 20, 22–25; communication, 2, **3**, 19–20, 106; grooming, 2–3, 16; learned skills, 23, 35; nocturnal, 7, **57**, 115; swimming, **2**, **18**, 23, 31, 33, 106; territorial, 21–22, 24–25, 74, 88
Belaney, Archibald. *see* Grey Owl
British Columbia, 80–81

cambium (bark), 7, 27, 114
Canada: beaver symbolism, 79, 87, 106; place-names, 59–61
canals, **50**–51, **55**, 114
capybara, 14
Castor canadensis. *see* North American beaver
castoreum, 21–22, 114
Castor fiber. *see* Eurasian beaver
castorids, 6, 8–**9**, 114
Chile, beavers in, 72
China, beavers in, 72
Chu, Wenwen, 72
citizen science, 48-49, 112, 114
climate change, 77, 86
Collier family, 80–81
colony, 20, 22–25, 64, 114
communication, 2, **3**, 19–20, 106
conservation: coexistence, 88-95, 99, 101, 110; reintroduction, 72, 74-77, 101, 115; relocation, **76**, 88, 95–98; research, 32–33, 42–43, 48–49;

trapping regulations, 66, 71; wildlife rescue, 17, **113**
culverts, 84, 93–94, 114

diet, 7, **26**, 27–28, **104**
DNA, 5-6, 114
dogs, 84–85, 105
ducks, 56

ecosystem, 52–56, 91, 93, 114
ecosystem engineer, 1, 10, 114
Elk River Alliance, 110
Eurasian beaver, 5–6, 61–62, 72, **73**

fish, **43**, 55, 87, 103
flow devices, **90**, **92**-94, 110
food: diet, 7, **26**, 27–28, **104**; droppings, 28; stored as fat, 32
food caches, **13**, 23, **30**–32, 39, 106, 114
Forbes, Doris, 17
fossils, 8–**9**
frogs, **55**, 87
fur, 2–3, 15–**16**, 23, 32-33, 61, **65**
fur trade, 61–**67**

giant beavers, 8, **9**
Goulstone, Garrett, 48–49
Grey Owl, 68–71, 78, 107
groundwater, 87, 114

habitat: beaver, **48**-49, 89, 97, 101; created for other species **43**, 53-**57**, 85; defined, 115

hats, **61**-62
herons, 55, **57**
Heter, Elmo (Scotty), **74**, 75
Hood, Glynnis, 32, 33, 50–51
humans, conflict with beavers, **6**, **25**, 83–85, 88, 90–94

Idaho, beavers in, 74–75, 77
incisors, 8, 11, **65**, 84, 115
Indigenous Peoples, 3, 7, 60-66, 68, 76, 80-81
International Beaver Day, 107, 108, 113

juveniles, 19, 23-25, 32, 74

keystone species, 1, 52–56, 115
kits, 13, 17, 19-20, 22–**24**, 60

life-span, 25
Lisle, Skip, 93–94
lodges: bank lodges, **13**; building of, 32, 40-41, 45–**47**; defined, 115; design, **13**–14, inside, **20**, 24, 32-33

Martinez Beaver Festival, **66**, 90–91, **109**
Methow Beaver Project (MBP), 95–98, **111**
Milligan, Madeleine, 110
Montana Conservation Corps (MCC), 48–49
moose, **54**, 55
Mott, Ava, 95, 96
muskrats, 32–33

Newhouse, Sewell, 63
Newman, Ila, 95, 98

New York, beavers in, 79
nocturnal activity, 7, 20, **36**, 44, 115
North American beaver, 5-7

Oregon flag, 62

Perryman, Heidi, 90–91
pet beavers, 17, 44, 70–71
plankton, 55, 115
ponds: ecology of, 53–56, 81, 86–87; making, 10, 39, **44**; in winter, 30–31
population, 6–7, 64, 72, 77–79
predators, 10–11
Prince Albert National Park (SK), 70, 78
public awareness: education, 70–71, **84**, 112; and festivals, **66**, 90–91, 107–**109**; resources, 116–117

range of beavers, 6-7
reintroduction, 72, 74-77, 101, 115
relocation, **76**, 88, 95–98
Richards, Dorothy, 107–108
Rybczynski, Natalia, 8, **9**

sand-paint, 99, 111
scent mounds, **21**, 106
Sino-Mongolian beaver, 72
Skagit River Delta (WA), 43

tail, **3**, 18, 19–20, **31**, 32, 106
teeth, **9**, **18**, 65
territorial behaviors, 21–22, 24–25, 74, 88
Thie, Jean, 42, **60**

Thompson, David, 42
tracks, **106**
trees: cambium (bark), 7, 27, 114; cutting of, **7**, 35–**38**, 83; planting of, **89**, 101; preferred species, 22, 27; protection, 91, 99, 101, 111; in wetlands, 55–56
Tulalip Beaver Project (WA), **76**
turtles, **53**, 55

urban beavers, 78–79, 83–84, 89–91, **105**

Vancouver (BC), beavers in, **78**
voles, 33, 55

Washington State, beavers in, **76**, 95–98
water lilies, **26**, 27, **34**
water table, 86-87, 103, 115
wetlands, **42**, 53–56, **78**, 87, 110
Wilde, Emily, **103**
wildlife rescue centers, 113
willow, 22, 27, **89**, 91, 101
wire-wrapping trees, 91, 99, 101, 111
wolves, 10, 78
Wood Buffalo National Park (AB), 42, 43
woodpeckers, 55–56

The author with a life-size model of a giant beaver at the Yukon Beringia Interpretive Centre in Whitehorse, Yukon. FRANCES BACKHOUSE

FRANCES BACKHOUSE studied biology in university and worked as a park naturalist and a biologist before becoming an environmental journalist and author. Her other books include *Once They Were Hats: In Search of the Mighty Beaver* and *Children of the Klondike*, which won the 2010 City of Victoria Butler Book Prize. She lives in Victoria, British Columbia, with her partner, Mark, who is also a writer. Frances loves exploring the natural world both close to home and far away, especially when it involves camping. If she comes across beavers during an outing, it's even better.